Peer-to-Peer Lending with Chinese Characteristics

Literature on China's finance in the West has focused on "financial repression" in its highly regulated financial markets. However, fundamental changes in China's financial system are underway and China's peer-to-peer (P2P) lending is now the largest in the world.

This book uses exclusive research, interviews and surveys to bring readers a clear picture of the rapidly developing P2P lending industry in China. It is comprised of two parts. The first part is a comprehensive analysis of China's P2P lending industry. It outlines the factors behind the meteoric rise of P2P lending in China, and also the challenges its rapid rise has posed. The second part is a panoramic survey of China's P2P lending industry with studies of typical cases, which also provide reference to the analysis in the first part. In addition, it introduces the existing relevant regulations, regulators and likely upcoming regulatory measures, as well as the diverse body of new financial institutions appearing with the development of the industry, in order to analyse in-depth the current functioning of the industry and its lending practices in China through a large scale survey.

Research Group Members

Martin Chorzempa was a Fulbright Scholar and researcher at the Association of German Banks. As a Luce Scholar at Peking University and China Finance 40 Forum (CF40), he researched Chinese financial reforms. He is currently a Masters in Public Administration in International Development candidate at the Harvard Kennedy School.

Kai Guo is Deputy Director-General of the International Department at the People's Bank of China and was an economist at the International Monetary Fund. He holds a PhD degree in economics from Harvard University and his research interests include international finance, macro economics, and the Chinese economy. His most recent book is *Mr. Wang's Tale of Economics* (2012), a national bestseller in economics in China.

Feng Guo is a research fellow at Shanghai Finance Institute (SFI) and a postdoctoral fellow at the Institute of Internet Finance at Peking University. He received a PhD in economics from Fudan University and has published extensively in leading academic journals in China. Recently he has spent much time researching China's P2P industry.

Qianzheng Wang is a research associate at CF40. He earned his Bachelor of Arts in Economics from Renmin University of China, a Master of Applied Economics from City University of Hong Kong, and a Master of Economics from Simon Fraser University in Canada.

Chief Translators
Sam Overholt
Tao Mengying

The "New Finance Book Series" was created by the Shanghai Finance Institute (SFI). The book series traces developments in new finance, explores new trends, pursues solutions to novel problems, and inspires new knowledge.

Shanghai Finance Institute (SFI) is a leading non-governmental, non-profit research institute dedicated to policy research in the cutting edge fields of finance. SFI was established on July 14th, 2011, and operates under the guidance of the China Finance 40 Forum (CF40), in strategic cooperation with the Shanghai Huangpu District government.

China Finance 40 Forum (CF40) is a non-governmental, non-profit and independent think tank dedicated to policy research in the fields of macro economics and finance. CF40 operates as a "40×40 club" with about 40 influential experts around the age 40.

In addition, research in this report also received academic support from CFCITY. **CFCITY** is a high-level training institute created under the CF40 in cooperation with innovative financial leaders from government, business and academia. It provides professional and cutting edge training for financial institutions, and develops a pool of talents with global perspectives, deep understanding of modern financial business and risk management proficiency.

Peer-to-Peer Lending with Chinese Characteristics

Development, regulation and outlook

P2P Research Group

Shanghai Finance Institute

LONDON AND NEW YORK

First published 2017
by Routledge

2 Park Square, Milton Park, Abingdon, Oxfordshire OX14 4RN
52 Vanderbilt Avenue, New York, NY 10017

Routledge is an imprint of the Taylor & Francis Group, an informa business

First issued in paperback 2020

British Library Cataloguing in Publication Data
A catalogue record for this book is available from the British Library

Library of Congress Cataloging-in-Publication Data
A catalog record has been requested for this title

ISBN: 978-1-138-23459-8 (hbk)
ISBN: 978-0-367-51667-3 (pbk)

Typeset in Times New Roman
by Apex CoVantage, LLC

Contents

Figures and table

Figures

Table

Appendix

Introduction

Chinese peer-to-peer lending (P2P) is now the largest in the world by far, at over $53 billion in loans intermediated in 2014.[1] This rapid financial development might seem surprising, as the typical view among China watchers has been that finance has lagged behind development in other sectors and is dominated by large, state-owned banks. Literature on Chinese finance in the West has focused on "financial repression" in its highly regulated financial markets, but fundamental changes in China's financial system are underway. These changes have weakened existing regulations and opened up the playing field to a diverse body of new financial institutions.

This report comprises two parts. The first part is a comprehensive analysis of China's P2P industry. In this part, we analyze the factors that led to the explosive growth of P2P in China, including a long history of interpersonal lending, thriving informal finance, an immense buildup in household wealth, and limited investment channels. Then, we outline the P2P market in China and associated issues, including credit rating and guarantees. Third, we outline the existing regulations, regulators, and likely upcoming regulatory measures. Fourth, we predict how this industry will evolve and explore the role it will play in the broader Chinese financial system. The second part is a panoramic survey of China's P2P industry. By analyzing comprehensive data and typical cases, the survey evaluates the development and risks of P2P platforms in China and provides reference to the analysis in the first part.

The analysis in the first part was authored by Martin Chorzempa. The survey in the second part was conducted by Dr. Guo Feng and Wang Qianzheng from Shanghai Finance Institute (SFI). Dr. Guo Kai provided advice on the research and analysis throughout the book.

Note

1 Source: Payments and Clearing Association of China. http://www.crowd fundinsider.com/2015/05/68230-china-association-of-payment-settlement-places-number-of-p2p-platforms-at-over-2300/

Peer-to-peer lending with Chinese characteristics

Development, regulation and outlook

1   What is P2P and how is Chinese P2P different?

Individuals have been lending to each other since at least the beginnings of recorded history. Shopkeepers make sales on credit, sovereigns borrow from subjects, and people make loans to friends who fall on hard times. If interpersonal lending has such a long history, why is there suddenly such a hype surrounding P2P? What is new about it this time around? These are the questions this section endeavors to answer.

The first peer-to-peer platform, Zopa, was founded in 2005 in the UK. Its name provides a clue to the growth seen worldwide by the industry: Zopa stands for "zone of positive agreement," a term used in negotiation to represent the range of possible transactions agreeable to all parties. The key difference between this new P2P and previous interpersonal lending is that the borrowers and lenders no longer need to know each other or share a common association other than being connected by the platform. Previous transactions were based on mutual trust, but trust is both difficult and costly to build. Potential transactions were thus undertaken mostly between members of the same community.

The Internet platforms eliminated these restrictions by providing credit evaluation and creating transactions in the zone of positive agreement between potential borrowers and lenders that would never have occurred under the old system. Since then, the industry has enjoyed exponential growth in the US, UK, and especially China. China's heavily regulated, state-dominated banking sector may not seem at first glance to be a fitting breeding ground for financial innovation, but these factors are precisely why it has become so large compared to other countries. The creativity of Chinese entrepreneurs in finding regulatory gaps has built a new industry seemingly out of thin air.

It would take an encyclopedia-length book to outline the thousands of unique business models Chinese P2P platforms are employing, but they are all variations on the same theme. These firms use the Internet to turbocharge a section of China's legal code that permits interpersonal lending. They then take it far beyond its intended scope of two individuals in the same locality lending to one another. The basic model is a web-based platform where borrowers apply for loans that then are sold to investors on the site. The platform charges a commission and profits from the difference between interest rates charged to the borrower and paid to the lender. The model up until this point will be familiar to anyone knowledgeable about P2P lending in the US or Europe, but it does not end there.

The platforms offer investors "guarantees," often of both principal and interest, backed by the platform itself, a financial institution, or a guarantee company about which the investors know little to nothing. To elderly retail investors with low-yielding savings in the bank, high, guaranteed returns sound like a deal almost too good to be true. The platforms regularly and invisibly pay out their own funds to reimburse investors for any losses, making defaults "disappear." The loans are also of very short duration, around three to six months, so borrowers likely have to roll over the loans continually, paying hefty fees each time around. Aggressive advertising campaigns recruit both lenders and borrowers with promises of special promotional rates and gifts. The effective interest rates are often far above the legal limit of four times the official benchmark rate, but this appears to be a minor obstacle. Borrowers range from couples arranging a wedding they cannot yet afford to medium-sized listed companies looking to expand. Another key characteristic is that mismatches in the amount of loans investors want to buy and borrowers want to take out are smoothed by the platforms, who give loans themselves if there are not enough lenders and find alternative investment projects if there are not enough borrowers. In short, they are banks in all but name and regulation. Most of these characteristics would be illegal for banks in China and P2P firms in other countries, so how are they able to do this?

There was no specific regulation for online lending, and no government department had the legal authority to step in. The banking regulator and local finance departments could step in only if investors complained about loss of funds, the securities regulator saw no "securities" involved to oversee, and the central bank focused on payments operators. These firms were in an almost perfect regulatory vacuum. The government knew what was going on but sat on the sidelines and gave mildly positive statements while intently observing the industry's growth. This all changed with the release of regulatory principles from China's State Council in mid-July. Agencies are now empowered to regulate P2P firms, so many of the practices outlined earlier may disappear by the time this publication goes to press.

The accommodating stance up until recently followed the introduction and explosive growth of Yu'E Bao, Alibaba's revolutionary online money market account that is now China's largest mutual fund. Yu'E Bao allowed

Chinese with any amount of money in their e-commerce account to invest it, with redemption on demand and rates about double those prevailing in banks for *time* deposits. It could all be done on the millions of smartphones in every corner of China, exposing average Chinese to a new way of managing their money that skipped long lines in rigid, state-owned banks and financial repression.

While its growth has since slowed and the interest rates have come down, Yu'E Bao paved the way for Chinese P2P. An Internet-based product like this from a trusted, well-respected brand like Alibaba changed the Chinese consciousness and expanded the realm of possibility for financial products. The Yu'E Bao success story is in turn part of a longer term goal for government reformers: interest rate liberalization. The People's Bank of China (PBoC) has gradually allowed banks more flexibility in determining their deposit and lending rates at levels different from the benchmarks. At the same time, the development of China's interbank market, in which financial institutions like trust companies can also borrow, created a mostly market-driven interest rate for the first time in recent Chinese history. Yu'E Bao client funds could be invested in this market rather than in low-yielding bank deposits. Chinese retail investors now have a wide variety of financial products vying for their hard-earned Renminbi. These changes are not far off from those that occurred when money market funds were first introduced in the US as a reaction to interest rate controls. It is into this environment that Chinese P2P was born.

It is important to note that the author uses the term "P2P" here solely for convenience. Chinese sources tend to use P2P interchangeably with other terms that mean "online lending," and the US and Europe have now coalesced around the term "marketplace lending" as more inclusive than "peer-to-peer." P2P has often been understood to be individual-to-individual, which would not accurately describe the lending on platforms like Lending Club and Prosper now mostly funded by institutional investors. It also would not accurately describe the thousands of new entrants to the online lending market in China, which have expanded their lines of business into business credit, wealth management, asset exchanges, information provision, credit rating, and many more. In this report, the author therefore will use the terms "online lending," "marketplace lending," and "P2P" interchangeably to more broadly include loans made over platforms that connect borrowers and lenders.[1]

Note

1 This definition is suggested by Foundation Capital. http://blog.lendit.co/the-evolution-of-p2p-lending-a-new-frontier-for-finance/

2 Why does P2P exist in China?

Chinese P2P has taken off, leaving US and UK marketplace lending in the dust. In 2014, the China Payments and Clearing Association estimated total P2P lending at $53.76 billion. By contrast, the UK industry association P2PFA estimates the UK total at just under $1.9 billion in 2014, and Foundation capital estimated 2014 US marketplace lending at $8.8 billion.[1] With such a new industry involving many smaller players, there is bound to be a large margin of error in these estimations, but even so, Chinese P2P appears to be doing about five times the volume of its counterparts in the US and UK combined. Although the first P2P platform in China was founded two years after Prosper emerged in the West, since 2006–2007 Chinese P2P growth has outpaced others. To understand why P2P has thrived in China, we need to understand the context behind it in different aspects: cultural, economic, and technical.

Technical progress is laying the foundation

Technology is the backbone of P2P as well as its main competitive advantage versus more established financial institutions. The most important technical requirement for P2P to gain rapid adoption is Internet usage, which provides a low-cost marketing and distribution channel for platforms as well as the necessary sources of data for credit rating. Although the Internet came late to China, its adoption has been rapid, especially for mobile Internet. Official statistics as of December 2014 from the China Internet Information Center puts mobile Internet users at 557 million, which puts China's online population larger than the entire population of Europe or the US.

Even more interesting is that mobile users make up over 85% of total Internet users in China. Smartphones are everywhere. In the author's experience, even rural areas of Tibet, one of China's poorest and sparsely inhabited provinces, provided reliable 3G coverage, meaning even a shepherd could apply for loans and invest funds through a P2P platform despite being many days' journey from the closest bank branch. All someone would need is a smartphone. Although these numbers are large, they have the potential to become far larger in the coming years. According to the Internet Society, China's Internet penetration rate is 45.8%, putting it in 86th place, behind countries like Moldova and Trinidad and Tobago.[2] But China is unlikely to remain 86th for long.

An often-essential piece of the infrastructure required to run a P2P platform in China is third party payments. P2P platforms tend to be registered and regulated as informational intermediaries or asset exchanges, but parts of their business model such as guarantees and loan loss reserves mean that many are effectively credit intermediaries. One of the greatest legal risks for P2P operators has been being declared "illegal fundraisers," a conviction that could mean a figurative death sentence for their companies as well as a literal death sentence for those convicted of the crime. One way to reduce this risk is to route investor funds and borrower payments through third parties to reduce ambiguity about how who is raising funds.

In fact, just like the P2P industry today, the third party payments industry operated in a legal limbo for about 12 years, beginning in 1999 but taking off after Alibaba's launch of its Alipay service to facilitate online shopping transactions on its Taobao platform at the end of 2004. Alipay and 26 other companies received licenses for third party payments services on 26 May 2011, which marked the beginning of clearer regulatory rules for the industry.[3] According to iResearch, Internet payments reached 2.4 trillion RMB in value in Q1 2015, up almost 30% year-on-year. While 24.3% of these payments were for online shopping, a large and growing share of 18.9% went to funds like Alibaba's Yu'E Bao. Alibaba is the clear market leader in third party payments with its Alipay product, now at 48.9% market share. The second place player, Tencent with Tenpay, reached just under 20% of the market by transaction value.[4]

Although a few large players dominate the market, the long tail of the industry has also grown rapidly, buoyed by a stream of licenses provided by the central bank for new entrants to the market. By July 2014, the PBoC had issued 269 licenses for third party payments providers.[5] Some of these providers, like Huifutianxia, offer specialized account management services to P2P companies. These third party services have facilitated the market entry for P2P platforms, as each does not need to build its payments and account management infrastructure from scratch. It also provides more support to the platforms' assertion that they do not function as credit intermediaries. Platforms claim that they do not touch funds managed by the third parties, including any loan loss reserve funds.

Another benefit to the migration of payments online is the creation of data that can be used for credit rating. Since only the 300 million or so Chinese who have credit cards from banks have sufficiently informative credit histories, platforms in China have struggled with a paucity of data from which one can create risk models, an issue less salient in the United States due to its long history of consumer credit and well-established credit bureaus. Some platforms worry about the concentration of this data at third party payments providers (which may have data from numerous client platforms) and the risk that this may lead the payments companies to enter the market as competitors themselves.

Third-party payments have also led to broader public acceptance of online, mobile financial services. Alipay reported over 300 million real-name registered users, implying that over 50% of Chinese mobile Internet users had an account.[6] If one feels secure making payments by phone, why not lend, invest, or borrow as well?

However, not all platforms are continuing to use these relatively new payments providers for their account management, and most P2P firms will move to banks. In 2014 and 2015, some of the larger platforms eschewed third party payment services and instead placed their accounts at banks like Minsheng or Citic Bank.[7] Why would a platform choose a more costly, much more highly regulated solution to manage their accounts? One reason is that in a crowded field with tens of new platforms being created every day and tens failing, with no standardized disclosure, working with a bank sends a strong signal about the risk management and reliability of a platform. This signal then in turn may provide the platform with a comparative advantage in marketing to China's stability minded investors. The 10 regulatory agencies' 18 July 2015 guiding opinions on the development of Internet finance established a requirement for third party bank custodians on accounts, which will cause further migration toward bank account management. We will examine this and other areas of regulation in a later section of this book.

In sum, China's rapid technological development has provided a strong basis for P2P companies' existing position and future growth. Internet penetration, though low as a percentage of the population, is rising rapidly. With this rise come hundreds of millions of new potential customers for online lenders as well as new sources of data to evaluate credit risk. Other financial innovations like third party payments have allowed P2P to reduce their risk of running afoul of illegal fundraising laws.

Government policy is helping push Internet finance

In March 2015, the Chinese government unveiled its official "Internet plus" strategy that clearly supports the development of P2P and e-commerce more broadly. The strategy aims to drive economic growth by developing the combination of Internet technology like big data with manufacturing and commerce. The accompanying investment in Internet infrastructure will get more people online as well as improve speeds and cut costs for those who already have access, expanding the potential market for online P2P platforms. For example, in May, Premier Li Keqiang called on mobile providers to make mobile data cheaper and faster. They responded almost immediately with 20–35% cuts in mobile Internet speeds, a move which will put mobile Internet closer to reach for the poorest sectors of the population like migrant workers and small-scale farmers.[8]

Local governments have also been eager to attract Internet finance businesses like P2P to their jurisdictions. Shanghai was the first to roll out supportive policies, but seven other cities followed, including Beijing and Shenzhen, in 2014. For example, Shanghai's municipal government launched an Internet Finance Park in 2014 and filled the space with companies like Dianrong in only three months. In August 2014, it issued official support measures for Internet finance companies, including tax incentives and streamlining certain types of registration.[9] The accommodative attitudes both the central and local governments have taken toward Internet finance broadly have had a powerful effect in encouraging companies to enter the industry. It signals official recognition of P2P's legitimacy and recognition of its long-term potential.

The economics are right for P2P

Economic factors, both at the household level and for businesses, have contributed to healthy supply and demand for P2P loans. Among households, the proportion needing credit is high, and the search for yield among wealthier households has provided ample funds as P2P gains wider acceptance. For businesses, the growth in private enterprise and entrepreneurship has created a need for business loans, often smaller loans than banks tend to provide.

Households need better credit and investment opportunities

The conventional wisdom in the West about Chinese households as thrifty savers with little need for credit and low consumption, investing solely in homes and bank deposits, hides a much more complicated reality. In fact, this reality is ideal for the development of P2P. The China Household Finance Survey results indicated in 2012 that around 50% of surveyed households reported consumption either equal to or larger than their income.[10] This result implies an enormous demand for credit from the 650 million or so Chinese who would by implication be net borrowers. Of the rest of the population, though they may be net lenders, many millions will still take out loans for mortgages, tuition, cars, and other large purchases. In fact, 50% of Chinese households reported owning less than 405,000 RMB in assets, or about 65,000 USD. Since this includes housing assets, these households would likely need to borrow to cover unexpected expenses or make large purchases. Since banks have only a limited capacity to expand lending and tend to prefer large loans to state-owned enterprises, many of these consumers could turn to P2P.

Businesses need capital to continue growing

Both supply and demand for capital are growing rapidly in China, which has created borrower and investor needs that the giant state-owned banks have not satisfied. In the past, when state planners ran China's economy, the government budget would allocate capital directly to businesses according to the economic plan, and any "profits" by state-owned enterprises would be remitted directly back to the central government. China's households had little capital of their own, and private business was discouraged if not outright forbidden, especially during the Cultural Revolution from the mid-1960s to the mid-1970s. Reform and opening revolutionized China's economy, creating both an enormous stock of household wealth and profitable investment opportunities.

We can see the rapid growth in Chinese private business since China joined the World Trade Organization in 2001. The decade from 2002–2012 saw the number of registered private enterprises in China more than quadruple from 2.6 million to 10.9 million and individual businesses almost double from 23.8 million to 40.6 million.[11] The China Household Finance Survey notes that in 2014, 14.1% of the Chinese population was self-employed, almost double the US's 7.2%. Such small businesses are either underserved by existing official financial institutions or not served at all, and are thus ideal customers for P2P platforms. In a survey of entrepreneurs in Henan province, Kellee Tsai found that 93% never had bank loans, but 60% had obtained credit from non-banks.[12] The rise of private business needs capital, and the millions of individual businesses who were previously unable to get credit from banks can now turn to P2P.

Interest rate controls and liberalization

The famously high savings rate in China is actually driven by the large proportion of income for those in the upper reaches of the income distribution and companies. With slowing housing price growth, a volatile stock market, and low interest rates for deposits, the stable, high investment yield offered by P2P is very attractive, often much higher than comparable wealth management products offered by banks and trust companies. Lower minimum investments as low as 100 Yuan attract investors who may lack the investable funds to reach investment thresholds for investments in wealth management products and trust products. A comparison with the US shows just how much room Chinese households may have to diversify their financial assets. US households held only 12.7% of their financial assets in bank savings, but the corresponding share for Chinese households was almost 58%.[13] Cash was another large component at 17.93%, meaning that over 75% of Chinese household financial assets were invested in products with either low or no yield. Hopefully P2P can help these households gain a better return on their hard-earned savings.

One by-product of China's highly regulated banking system has been financial repression of Chinese households. The Chinese central bank sets benchmark deposit and lending rates for banks, from which rates offered can deviate by set amounts. While permitted deviations from official rates increased since the early 2000s, amounting to some de facto rate liberalization, these rates are still very low in 2016. Lardy calculates that average real deposit rates in China from 2002–2008 was –.3%, and that real demand deposit rates in mid-2008 were –7.18% as the benchmark rate failed to rise with inflation. He estimates that earning real rates similar to those in 2002 (still far below today's P2P rates) would have netted Chinese savers an extra 690 billion RMB more for the first half of 2012 alone.[14] Clearly there is an unmet need for both loans and investment products that P2P is ideally suited to fill.

Chinese culture: a history of interpersonal lending

Finally, Chinese culture surrounding lending is one explanation for the explosive growth of the industry. This culture is rooted in thousands of years of Chinese individuals and businesses lending between one another rather than through banks. This phenomenon is especially pronounced in rural areas, which until very recently made up the vast majority of Chinese society. Results from the Southwest University of Finance and Economics' Chinese Household Finance Survey show that this informal lending dominates official financial institutions in rural areas, and banks are in the minority even in urban areas where visiting a bank branch is much easier.

Among rural households surveyed in 2012, 48.3% reported using informal finance to borrow, but only 14.1% reported loans from official institutions. Urban household numbers were 28% and 15.9%, respectively. These informal lenders comprise a vast world of credit providers at highly varied interest rates and legality. Much informal lending for rural households has been at either low or no interest, lent between friends and family.[15] The shared social bonds and likely deep knowledge of the others' finances allowed both an assessment of repayment risk and a powerful social incentive to repay.

Just as in every society, the Chinese also have high-interest lenders who would be called "loan sharks" in the West. In 2012, 11.9% of households reported lending money directly themselves, while 33% borrowed money, over 1/3 of which was for business or agriculture. Such borrowing comes at a high cost; the average rate paid by rural informal borrowers was 26.47%.[16]

This cultural predilection for interpersonal lending applies to companies as well, though regulation means they generally need to go through banks. *The Wall Street Journal* estimated that China's 10 largest banks brokered 3.7 trillion RMB in so-called "entrusted loans" in 2013, in which Chinese companies lend to each other in a deal organized through banks.[17] In these transactions, the bank functions somewhat like a P2P platform would. Its own capital is not supposed to be at risk, and the loans do not show up on their own balance sheet.

Unlike in the West, well-established cultural norms around lending by individuals and companies in China accelerated the acceptance of investors and lenders for P2P. It is one of the reasons retail investors dominate Chinese P2P, while in the West it is institutional investors doing so.

Notes

1 "Strong Growth Continues in Peer-To-Peer Lending Market." 30 April 2015. http://p2pfa.info/strong-growth-continues-in-peer-to-peer-lending-market Accessed 27 June 2015.
2 Internet Society Global Internet Maps: Internet User Penetration. http://www.internetsociety.org/map/global-internet-report/ Accessed 27 June 2015.
3 Alibaba announced it received a license in late May of 2011. Source: "Alipay Gets Licence to Set Up E-Payment System." *Reuters*. 26 May 2011. http://www.reuters.com/article/2011/05/26/us-alipay-idUSTRE74P26120110526 Accessed 27 June 2015.
4 "iResearch Views: Q1 2015 China Third-Party Internet Payment GMV Attain 2.4 Tn Yuan 4 June 2015." *iResearch*. http://www.iresearchchina.com/views/6472.html Accessed 15 June 2015.
5 "Central Bank Issues More Third-Party Payment Licenses." *Caixin*. 16 July 2014. http://english.caixin.com/2014–07–16/100705011.html Accessed 27 July 2015.
6 As of 8 February 2014. http://ab.alipay.com/i/dashiji.htm Accessed 27 July 2015.
7 "P2P Lenders Partner with China Minsheng Bank to Manage & Safeguard Investor Funds." *Crowdfund Insider*. 14 February 2015. http://www.crowdfundinsider.com/2015/02/62747-p2p-lenders-partner-with-china-minsheng-bank-to-manage-safeguard-investors-funds/ Accessed 2 July 2015.
8 "China's Telcoms Heed Premier Li Keqiang's Call to Slash Internet Fees." *South China Morning Post*. 17 May 2015. http://www.scmp.com/news/china/economy/article/1799149/chinas-telcos-heed-premiers-call-cut-internet-fees Accessed 17 May 2015.
9 "Shanghai Pledges Support for Internet Finance." *China Daily*. 8 August 2015. http://usa.chinadaily.com.cn/business/2014–08/08/content_18276025.htm Accessed 3 July 2015.

10 Gan, Li, "Findings from the Chinese Household Finance Survey." Southwestern University of Finance and Economics. September 2012. http://chfs.swufe.edu.cn/upload/files/Report-English-Sep-2012–2.pdf Accessed 29 July 2015.
11 Lardy, Nicholas, 2015. "Markets Over Mao." Peterson Institute for International Economics, Washington, DC. P. 70.
12 Tsai, Kellee, 2001. "Beyond Banks: The Local Logic of Informal Finance and Private Sector Development in China." http://www.hks.harvard.edu/m-rcbg/Conferences/financial_sector/BeyondBanks.pdf Accessed 18 June 2015.
13 Ibid.
14 Lardy, Nicholas, 2012. "Sustaining China's Economic Growth after the Crisis." Peterson Institute for International Economics, Washington, DC.
15 Guo, Pei and Guangwen He, 2005. "Estimation on the Aggregate of China's Rural Informal Finance." Center for Rural Finance and Investment Research, China Agricultural University, Beijing.
16 Gan, Li, "Findings from the China Household Finance Survey." Southwest University of Finance and Economics, Sichuan. September 2012. http://chfs.swufe.edu.cn/upload/files/Report-English-Sep-2012–2.pdf Accessed 27 June 2015.
17 "Entrusted Lending Raises Risks in Chinese Finance." *The Wall Street Journal.* 1 May 2014. http://www.wsj.com/articles/SB10001424052702304163604579531383712290244 Accessed 29 June 2015.

3 An overview of Chinese P2P today

Platforms

P2P in China is currently a "wild-west" of finance. Tens of firms come online and tens more fail every month, loan intermediation has skyrocketed, and regulations seem to be a minimal constraint. In their report on the first half of 2015, Online Lending House and Yingcan Group put the number of operating platforms at 2,028 by the end of June 2015.[1]

Just under 900 of these platforms came online in the first six months of 2015 alone, and 73 leading platforms have already intermediated 500 million RMB or more.[2] According to these statistics, Guangdong's Hongling Capital intermediated just short of 13 billion RMB in June and July of 2015. To put this in international perspective, the loans intermediated by this one platform in the last two months is approximately equal to the total intermediated by the UK's entire P2P industry in 2014.

But with the proliferation of business models, such as that of CreditEase that focus on sourcing borrowers and investors offline, the data from Online Lending House may be missing significant amounts of P2P loans originating offline but still going through P2P platforms. For example, CreditEase works with Fair Isaac Corporation's (FICO) cloud-based Alternative Lending Platform but originates the vast majority of its loans through an offline sales force. Its P2P platform Yirendai is only a part of a massive company. It also maintains and staffs centers across China. In April 2015, a CreditEase representative informed the author that it is now present in 180 cities and 40 rural areas, with plans to expand into 1,000 rural areas from 2015–2020. It certainly has been active in hiring. In May 2015, CreditEase reported a total workforce of 46,000 employees.[3] Although it has such a large footprint and has been reported by companies like Lend Academy to intermediate loans of $6 billion in 2014 (see following table), Online Lending House only reports its loans through its online Yirendai platform, putting it at fourth place after Lufax, Hongling Capital, and Renrendai. The expansion of P2P companies into wealth management and a plethora of other services means

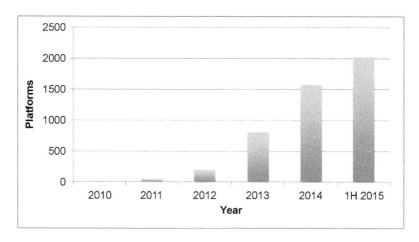

Figure 3.1 Operating platforms
Source: Online Lending House

Table 3.1 Top 10 largest P2P firms in 2014

1	CreditEase	China	$6,000
2	Lending Club	US	$4,400
3	Lufax	China	$2,300
4	Prosper	US	$1,600
5	SoFi	US	$1,300
6	OnDeck	US	$1,200
7	CAN Capital	US	$1,000
8	Avant	US	$500
9	RateSetter	UK	$457
10	Funding Circle	UK	$432

Source: Lendit China Webinar, 5 June 2015.

one cannot use any single metric to compare platforms. Shanghai Finance Institute, China Finance 40 Forum, and CFCITY jointly conducted a survey of 19 platforms, of which 12 reported offline locations for credit checks and business development. Of those 12, the number of offline locations doubled from end 2013 to end Q1 2015, when they ranged from 2 to 512 locations. In fact, the fastest growing platform registered an astounding 15x growth rate over this period.

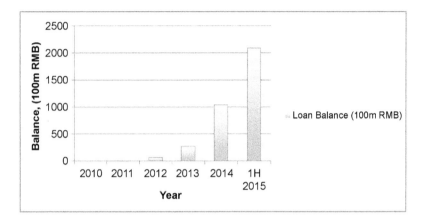

Figure 3.2 Loan growth is accelerating

Source: Online Lending House, Yingcan Group

Investor and loan characteristics

By the end of June 2015, P2P platforms had 2.18 million investors and 1.06 million borrowers. While that would be a large number of people for most countries, in China less than .2% of the population is an investor and less than .08% are borrowers. The room to grow this number remains enormous despite the already breakneck growth of P2P in China.

Loan intermediation growth has been rapid and accelerating. Chinese P2P loan balances have already doubled since the beginning of 2015 and stood at 200 billion RMB, or 32 billion USD at the end of June 2015.

By the end of Q1 2015, Online Lending House reported that 80% of P2P loans are concentrated in just four highly urban provinces: Guangdong, Zhejiang, Beijing, and Shanghai. The concentration in urban areas means P2P is still not reaching rural areas to the extent that should be possible with its electronic distribution methods, but expansion of rural Internet access should help drive growth in rural P2P lending going forward.

Average investor returns have been stable around 15% from 2013–2015. Maturities tend to be short, with an average of around six months, but almost 60% of loans mature in one to three months after issuance. Just as it is with wealth management products and bank loans, long-term loans from P2P are scarce; only 1.27% of loans were for one year or greater at the end of 2014. This is in contrast with Lending Club's focus on loans of three years or more. With such short maturities, it is likely that most borrowers depend

---

Box 1   Data Issues

Online Lending House obtains its data directly from P2P platforms and supplements that information with a team of researchers as well as collaboration with Yingcan Group for reports. The number quoted here is lower than that from the China Payment and Clearing Association cited in the introduction and measures total intermediation, not just loan balances. Therefore, the former would involve more double counting.

There are, however, concerns about the accuracy and completeness of the data from Online Lending House. For example, some experts informed the author that platforms have two sets of books: one for internal management and another that is "revised" for public consumption and reporting to Online Lending House. Outstanding loans could be overestimated due to exaggerated reporting by platforms but could also be underestimated because of lack of coverage of small regional platforms. Despite its flaws, it is one of the most comprehensive estimates for the industry, and is thus used here. The author anticipates that data quality will increase significantly after regulation mandates and standardizes disclosure.

---

on the ability to continue to roll over their loans, whether businesses or consumers. P2P companies report default rates below 2%, and one company the author interviewed that reported intermediating billions of RMB in loans even claimed they had never had a "bad debt."

Such claims seem impossible, but with no mandatory disclosure and no official definition of default, the P2P firms are for now free to post just about any number they wish. In a Q&A session with Lend Academy in March 2015, Lufax estimated its charge-off rate on unsecured loans at 4% and predicted a rate going forward of 6%.[4] One expert interviewed with direct knowledge of multiple platforms' loan performance estimated the true default numbers at 15% and potentially much higher for some less sophisticated platforms without effective risk management. In fact, default rates for originations have a different meaning depending on the firm's business model.

Although the loans may have relatively high default rate, third party guarantee companies and other financial institutions that backed the loans may step in to ensure that the P2P platform investors do not see any losses. Other small losses may be absorbed by loan loss reserves, and yet others may be hidden if the platform uses its own capital to pre-pay investors.

On secured loans, borrowers may default but forfeit collateral that can be sold for enough to reimburse investors in full. However, such repossessions are costly and often lengthy. The platform would need to decide whether to impose those costs on investors to show up as a sort of default, which is unlikely in the current environment. This differs from the US. For example, Lending Club makes it clear that any losses are borne by the investor and that funds collected later on overdue loans will be net of the expenses incurred by the loan servicer. There is hope that regulation will standardize disclosure for defaults in a way that allows us to analyze it, but even highly regulated Chinese banks have been accused of reporting impossibly low default numbers in the past, so this is not assured.

Fraud, failure, and gray market margin financing

The dark side of P2P has been insolvencies, failures, and outright frauds. In June 2015 alone, Online Lending House reported 125 new "problem platforms," 43 of which involved platform owners/managers running off with funds invested over the platform.[5] In total they report 786 problem platforms since 2011, of which almost half directly ran off with client money.

Some were scams from the very beginning. For example, Hubei's Shunchang Caifu[6] started in June 2015, registering capital for the business at 10 million RMB. It then attracted 222,000 RMB from 125 investors before taking down the site and running off less than a month into its operations.[7] Others like Jingyu Loans operated their platforms for not even a full day

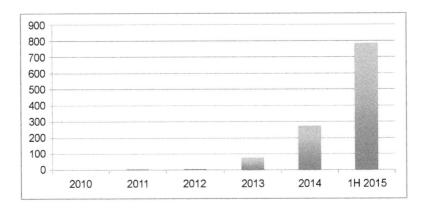

Figure 3.3 "Problem" platforms

Source: Online Lending House, Yingcan Group

before running off with client money.[8] Another scam targeted senior citizens, running off with over 100 million RMB.[9] These scams damage the reputation of the P2P industry as a whole. Coming regulation or self-regulation through industry associations with certification processes must find a way to reduce the prevalence of these scams to keep the industry on a healthy development track. The new regulation should give more resources, legal and human, to regulators to educate investors on how to avoid being cheated and shut down such illegal financing schemes before they can get large.

Another problem with P2P is the gray market financing many platforms have given speculators for stock buys, a problem that has found its way into the news since the stock market bubble burst. As the stock market began to rise amid a large expansion in margin lending, P2P firms began offering loans called "peizi," which roughly translates as "matching funds." Such loans skirted the leverage limits and other restrictions associated with margin borrowing from brokerages, allowing borrowers make sizable stock buys with little funds. For example, one could start with limited funds, borrow from Miniu98.com, post it with a stockbroker, receive official margin financing from the broker, and then buy stock. The leverage provided by the brokers would be limited to 50% equity, 50% debt, for example, for 500,000 RMB in stock one would have to have 250,000 in funds deposited with the broker. But the 50% leverage would hide the fact that the "equity" was not equity at all, rather debt from a different source.

This excessive leverage has since been blamed for some of the market's rapid rise and even more rapid fall, as a declining market leads to a vicious circle as lower prices forces liquidation of stock positions that then in turn lowers prices more. The China Securities Regulatory Commission has investigated Hundsun Technologies, a firm associated with Alibaba founder Jack Ma that ran a system connecting brokerages and firms like P2P platforms looking to extend margin loans. The Securities Regulator estimated that 2 trillion RMB in shadow margin financing went through this and other systems, with 500 billion RMB going through HOMS alone.[10] P2P firms linked up directly with brokerages without providing the real names of the investors, making it impossible to track the leverage of individual traders.[11] Due to backlash from regulators, P2P firms previously at the heart of this nexus like Miniu98.com are now abandoning the margin financing business,[12] but they could still face legal consequences and backlash for violating securities regulations.

Business models and guarantees

Chinese P2P companies' product offerings are distinguished from those offered to European or US customers in the volatility of returns, or lack thereof. The management of P2P companies in China explained to the author that this is due to a risk aversion shared by many Chinese investors. Volatility, most often due to visible defaults, makes it far more difficult to attract investors, so the platforms use a variety of methods to smooth out the returns. None of these methods would likely be permissible in the highly regulated US and European markets. One reason for the difference may be that the investor base for Chinese P2P is almost exclusively retail, while that of western "marketplace lenders" is now mostly institutional investors. Another is a lack of risk differentiation common across the Chinese financial system. Until recently, Chinese investors had access to a very limited set of options like bank deposits and stock investments. In contrast to the United States, few retail investors hold bonds, and money market accounts and wealth management products are all relatively new phenomena.

Some platforms like to put a portion of the interest paid, equivalent to about 3–6% of the loan balance, into a loan loss reserve fund. Platforms then maintain the funds in an account at a third party bank. When a borrower defaults or is late on his or her payments, the platform uses funds in the reserve to continue payments to the investor as if the borrower were not late.[13] The hope is that the delay is only temporary, and that resumption of payments or collections then replenish the reserve. Such a practice calls into question the platforms' stated role solely as "information intermediaries." Completely stable returns, promises of 100% safety, and pre-payment seem like a high-interest bank deposit, and would be difficult to differentiate for an average retail investor. For example, when asked what distinguished their product from a normal bank deposit, one platform manager pointed out that the formal lending party on the contract included every purchaser of the online investment product, rather than the platform itself.

Other platforms, like Jimu Box, use third party guarantee companies and other financial intermediaries to provide guarantees. A common business model is to accept borrowers on referral from these companies, which come with a guarantee of repayment if the borrower defaults. The management of Aitouzi noted in an interview that they cooperate with over 90 financial institutions for business. In fact, there are a plethora of companies who provide guarantees, including guarantee companies, factoring companies, financial leasing companies, and others. Though the regulation is not yet official, China Banking Regulatory Commission (CBRC) officials have stated that P2P firms should not use guarantee companies "linked" with themselves so the platforms are not themselves required to repay in the event of defaults. However, these distinctions, like many, are blurred in China. For example, the Lufax platform is part of the giant Ping An Insurance Group, whose credibility, brand recognition, and network has helped the platform grow rapidly. The guarantor for its loans also is part of Ping An, but Lufax management has insisted that it does not qualify as a "linked" guarantor because it is a separate legal entity.

Companies that have not used one of these methods have not fared as well. Paipaidai, the first P2P company in China, has not offered guarantees and runs a purely offline model. Despite being an early mover, it has grown more slowly than companies offering fixed returns. In October 2012, the *Financial Times* reported that CreditEase, with its extensive offline business and guaranteed returns had by then intermediated 2–3 billion USD in loans versus Paipaidai at 200 million RMB.[14]

While Chinese retail investors clearly prefer the guaranteed options, such models carry a great deal of risk, especially in the event of a sharp economic downturn. Without experiencing defaults, investors are unable to directly see the risks they are undertaking by investing in a high-interest product. Each company is careful to note that despite marketing materials with phrases such as "100% safe" and "guaranteed principal and interest," exhaustion of their loan loss reserves not make them legally liable to compensate investor losses from their own capital. Despite these assurances, multiple P2P companies have privately acknowledged that they occasionally make advances out of their own capital if large borrowers experience payment delays in order to maintain investor confidence. If the losses became large enough, it is easy to imagine a platform falling into bankruptcy after using up its capital to provide "advances" to investors.

The third party guarantee model is not without its flaws either. The third party guarantee industry is relatively young and often undercapitalized. For example, Hebei Financing Investment Guarantee Group Co. Ltd., a large state-owned guarantee company based in Hebei province that backed around 50 billion RMB in loans, suspended its business in April 2015. The provincial government founded it to back small and medium enterprise (SME) loans, but the worsening economy led to defaults that quickly exhausted the capital it had to back its guarantees, leaving P2P firms and other financial institutions with the dilemma of what to do with the defaults. It is yet to be seen who will ultimately be on the hook for the losses. More failures to pay by guarantee companies would put the P2P platforms in a bind, as they would have to decide whether to pass losses onto investors, which would risk shaking confidence in their platforms, and providing advances from their own funds, which would risk the solvency of the platform and potentially be illegal.

Credit rating

In discussions with industry participants and regulators, one of the most urgent worries about online lending is China's credit rating system. China's credit rating system became the largest in the world only three years after establishing its centralized system, and it had over 830 million entries in 2015.

China's first credit bureau was the still-operating Shanghai Credit Information Services (CIS), which started as a platform under the central bank that included data from state-owned banks in Shanghai. Banks were ordered to report all lending and credit events to CIS. The PBoC's credit rating data center depends on loans from banks for rating of individual and business credit. Interestingly, loans from other sources, like informal loans, small loan companies, pawn banks, and peer-to-peer lending companies are not included. Though the data is not complete, it is the most comprehensive nationwide source of data and is actually the largest credit system in the world with 830 million records for individuals.

For certain small business loans, Alibaba arguably has the most valuable data due to its dominance of the e-commerce field. It is certainly one of the few Chinese companies that can truly say it has access to "big data." Alibaba runs an online marketplace called Taobao and other platforms over which the vast majority of China's e-commerce runs. For any company whose business sells over these platforms, Alibaba has real-time access to its sales numbers as well as customer reviews that might provide an early warning that quality or service is slipping. On the basis of these metrics, as well as those it gains through its Alipay payments service, it can make almost instantaneous decisions on small loans to these companies.

Just as credit bureaus in the early days of the United States developed out of local and then regional groups of lenders, local credit evaluation companies have sprung up all across China. Such information sharing has grown in importance as the platforms operating in China expand both within jurisdictions and across them. The US market leader in credit scoring, FICO, has also entered the Chinese market aggressively. In June, *Bloomberg News* reported it already has over 40 customers for its Alternative Lending Platform, which allows companies like P2P platforms to analyze their loan book, rate credit, and also share some credit data using a cloud-based service.[15] FICO is used for the vast majority percentage of credit decisions in the US and is often touted prominently on P2P websites as a metric for the quality of its borrowers. It has, however, been the target of criticism in developed markets for its traditional approach to credit rating, which might seem to make it an odd partner for P2P. However, the lack of US-style credit bureaus in China has necessitated expansion into data sources for credit rating that include phone bills, third party payments operators, and even pawnshops, which are often not included in US credit reports.

Applications for loans on major Internet lending platforms require loan seekers to provide a scanned copy of their individual credit report from the central bank's system as part of their application, but P2P firms are not able to access the records directly themselves. Despite this, P2P platforms are often able to gain access to the records through cooperation with more established, licensed financial institutions with access, like guarantee companies with whom they collaborate. However, at the present, the lack of information sharing means an individual or business could potentially apply for loans at the same time from hundreds of P2P platforms, without it showing up on their credit report, a recipe for fraud and abuse. The lack of reporting also means low costs in the case of default, as unlike in the US it may well not show up on the credit report when applying for future loans. In the future, Chinese P2P will certainly need a centralized platform for loans to which it can report not only a "black list" of defaulters, but also loans issued and to whom. Only with comprehensive information sharing can P2P clamp down on this fraud and reduce "evergreening," whereby insolvent borrowers take out loans from one platform to pay back maturing debt.

Notes

1 "73 Platforms Reach Balances in Excess of 500 Million RMB, Numbers Double." *Online Lending House*. 1 July 2015. http://www.wangdaizhijia.com/news/hangye/20697-all.html Accessed 2 July 2015.
2 "73 Platforms Reach Balances in Excess of 500 Million RMB, Numbers Double." *Online Lending House*. 1 July 2015. http://www.wangdaizhijia.com/news/hangye/20697-all.html Accessed 2 July 2015.
3 "Happy 9th Birthday to CreditEase." *CreditEase Company News*. 28 May 2015. http://www.creditease.cn/news/gongsixinwen/2015/0528/2478.html Accessed 3 July 2015.
4 "Lufax: The World's Fastest Growing P2P Firm." *Lend Academy*. 27 March 2015. http://www.lendacademy.com/lufax-p2p-firm-china/ Accessed 5 July 2015.
5 Online Lending House Data: http://www.wangdaizhijia.com/zhuanti/sswd34/ Accessed 2 July 2015.
6 The first two characters are for a location, but are pronounced similarly to the Chinese word for "smooth" as in to go smoothly. Investors who lost funds may not appreciate the irony.
7 "Shunchang Caifu 2015–06–25 Hubei Changsha Closes Site and Cannot be Reached." *P2Peye*. http://www.p2peye.com/thread-430132–1–1.html Accessed 30 June 2015.
8 "National 'Problem' P2P Platforms Exceeds 100, Jingyu Loans Goes Online and Runs Off Same Day." *Netease Money*. 8 October 2014. http://money.163.com/14/1008/10/A81DD3CM00253B0H.html Accessed 30 June 2015.
9 "'Warm' Investment Company Runs Off, 300 Elderly Cheated out of Over 100 Million." *Online Lending House*. 3 July 2015. http://www.wangdaizhijia.com/news/hangye/20788.html Accessed 5 July 2015.
10 "China Stock Market Regulator Shines Light on Grey Market Financing." *South China Morning Post*. 14 July 2015. http://www.scmp.com/business/markets/article/1838672/china-stock-market-regulator-shines-light-grey-market-financing Accessed 26 September 2015.
11 "The Truth about HOMS Peizi." *Caijing*. 6 July 2015. http://magazine.caijing.com.cn/20150706/3919437.shtml Accessed 26 September 2015.

12 "P2P Lender Miniu98 Exits Margin Lending as Authorities Crack Down." *Global Times*. 13 July 2015. http://www.globaltimes.cn/content/931914.shtml Accessed 26 September 2015.

13 The platforms call this 垫付 (dian fu), roughly translated as an advance.

14 "China Needs a Robust Credit Infrastructure." *Financial Times*. 16 October 2012. http://www.ft.com/cms/s/0/fc84c4c8-0e13-11e2-8b92-00144feabdc0.html Accessed 3 July 2015.

15 "U.S. Credit-Score Firm FICO Betting on China Surge in P2P Loans." *Bloomberg News*. 17 June 2015. http://www.bloomberg.com/news/articles/2015-06-16/u-s-credit-score-firm-fico-betting-on-china-surge-in-p2p-loans Accessed 24 June 2015.

4   Regulation

One of the most difficult considerations for regulators is how to deal with industries undergoing rapid change and innovation like that of the P2P industry and Internet finance more broadly. The United States and China have not yet issued regulations specific to P2P, but the results have been night and day. It seems that existing regulations in the United States have been mostly sufficient in ensuring P2P platforms abide by the regulatory norms followed by more established financial institutions. For example, companies like Lending Club are subject to a thicket of national and state regulations.

US regulation

In the United States, platforms must ensure they are in compliance with a host of regulatory bodies. Federal provisions such as the Truth in Lending Act and others related to collections ensure P2P loans are able to meet stringent requirements for disclosure to borrowers when it comes to their final cost, including fees and interest. They also limit the actions creditors can undertake when a loan goes overdue and into collections.

State laws then add another layer of regulation. It is extremely difficult for platforms to issue loans and recruit investors in all states because each state has its own regulatory requirements and format for disclosures. Even formulas for calculation of expected annual percentage rate and finance charges can differ across states. Many states also have usury laws that set an upper limit on interest rates, though there are ways to "export" the lack of such limits if a bank registers in certain states like Utah. Since the loans are generally originated at banks, the issuing bank is subject to regulations by the FDIC and other bodies like the OCC.

Once the loan is issued, the platforms face disclosure requirements mandated by the SEC for the loan securitization. One of the few regulatory changes related to P2P in the US was SEC permission to issue a new type of security, and there was a real risk then that the application would be rejected. These regulations, mostly designed for traditional financial institutions facing retail investors with their own capital at risk have slowed the growth of marketplace lending in the US and added to compliance costs.

This regulatory environment is likely to grow only more difficult to navigate as the Consumer Financial Protection Bureau issues more regulations designed to protect those who borrow through the platforms, though its Project Catalyst and other measures are attempting to add flexibility and more informal ways of interacting with regulators. Numerous provisions of the Dodd-Frank Act have yet to come into play, as concrete rules for implementation by regulatory agencies are not settled. In short, despite not being designed for P2P, the US regulatory environment has generally ensured adequate disclosure and protected both investor and borrower interests.

UK regulation

Since 2014, the UK has arguably done the most to consciously encourage innovation through its regulatory framework. It has endeavored to create a streamlined regulatory environment that is far easier to navigate than that of the US. Originally, the Office of Fair Trading (OFT) regulated P2P platforms as consumer lenders, where separate regulation applied to activities related to "credit brokerage" and "credit intermediation," both of which are generally combined in P2P platforms.[1]

On 1 April 2014, regulatory responsibility was transferred to the Financial Conduct Authority (FCA), which created a specific category for P2P, called "operating an electronic system in relation to lending" that combined brokerage and intermediation to better fit the combination of these platforms' activities.[2] Six months later, in October 2014, it launched Project Innovate to "encourage innovation in the interest of consumers" and "promote competition through disruptive innovation."[3] To do this, it has reached out to industry participants to identify ways it can remove existing barriers to innovation arising from regulations and the way businesses interact with the regulators.

It has also proposed the creation of a "regulatory sandbox" (rolled out Spring 2016) that allows firms with a "genuine innovation" with "identifiable benefit[s] to consumers" to experiment with new activities in a "safe space" environment that protects them from certain regulatory consequences these activities normally would entail.[4] The FCA hopes this will allow more experimentation to get innovative products to market that otherwise might be withheld due to worries about possible regulatory action.

The FCA's regulation includes minimum capital requirements for platforms that consist of either a percentage of loaned funds or 50,000 GBP, whichever is greater. Firms must therefore keep the regulator up to date on the value of outstanding loans, which then allows the regulator to have a precise estimate of the total size of the market in a way that US or Chinese regulations do not yet make possible. Regulations also focus on the protection of client funds and servicing in the case of bankruptcy. Platforms must hold client funds in segregated accounts and submit detailed plans that ensure that the loans it has intermediated can easily continue to be serviced if it fails.[5]

Self-regulation also plays a role in the UK's P2P industry and has often led the introduction of government regulations. In 2011, the largest players banded together to create the P2PFA, or the Peer-to-Peer Finance Association, to agree on standards for self-regulation and lobby for regulations that benefit the industry. It requires members to avoid claiming its returns are "guaranteed," standardize calculation and disclose bad debt rates and returns, publish their updated loanbook, and ensure an orderly wind-down in the case of platform bankruptcy, among many other requirements available on the "operating principles" section of the P2PFA website.[6]

Chinese regulation and future directions for policy

China's P2P companies operated in a regulatory limbo until 18 July 18 2015, when the PBoC led an announcement from no less than 10 regulatory commissions titled "Guiding Opinions on Advancing the Healthy Development of Internet Finance." While not binding regulations in themselves, this document should be viewed as a foundation on which these agencies will build their more specific regulation and oversight. For example, P2P has been placed under the purview of the CBRC, but only a draft for public comment has been released at the time of this writing.

July's "Guiding Opinions" are the culmination of a debate about if, when, and how to regulate the industry. This debate began in earnest when P2P started its meteoric rise in 2013. Some worried that imposing specific regulation too early would choke off its development and reduce the capacity of market competition to differentiate platforms that are able to compete from those who will fail. Another issue is the capacity to regulate. China's financial regulatory system is separated into sometimes overlapping silos, with most regulatory responsibilities split between the "one bank and three commissions," including the central bank (PBoC), Banking Regulatory Commission (CBRC), Securities Regulatory Commission (CSRC), and Insurance Regulatory Commission (CIRC). These bodies make rules and implement legislation but also delegate certain responsibilities for implementation to local government offices. One example relevant to P2P is financial services offices in municipal governments who handle illegal fundraising cases.

However, P2P has challenged and outgrown this regulatory apparatus in its current form. These companies are operating seamlessly between lending, wealth management, leasing, insurance, payments, and many others, integrating them and easily crossing jurisdictions. How can a local government be expected to effectively regulate a company sourcing funds across the country for projects in numerous provinces? Adapting to the new reality will be one of the defining challenges of financial regulation in China for the coming years.

A senior policymaker explained to the author that once the government regulates P2P, it is also taking on responsibility for the industry in the eyes of ordinary people. The last thing regulators want is protests outside their offices and societal instability due to the collapse of a P2P platform. Despite over 600 platforms becoming "problem platforms" with solvency problems or fraud, this has not yet happened. Regulators will therefore tread lightly. Even if regulators were to find out that many of the smaller, less sophisticated platforms may well be insolvent as well due to higher than expected defaults and payments to clients out of platform capital, they may still be hesitant to intervene and face the ire of investors claiming that it was closed prematurely. In illegal fundraising cases, there generally needs to be a complaint from losing investors to justify government intervention, and Chinese P2P has yet to arrive at this situation at a large scale.

In fact, the hands-off approach in the initial stages is similar to that taken with shadow banking, which began to take off noticeably in 2011. It began on the margins or outside of the existing regulatory apparatus, but it grew rapidly to become a significant part of total social financing in China.[7] When policymakers understood it better and it grew large enough to pose risks to the broader financial system, they began to regulate it more strictly. Interestingly, the final rules and the division of responsibility for enforcing them were not made public. Though its growth has slowed, it is here to stay. P2P will likely follow in the same vein.

Although the government has put P2P platforms under the CBRC, it has only released general "guiding opinions," leaving the individual regulatory agencies to build on this foundation with specific rules. As of this writing, CBRC officials have made two main speeches outlining suggestions for the industry. On 21 April 2014, Liu Zhangjun, a CBRC official leading its office on illegal fundraising, laid out "red lines" for the industry, including:

1   Clarify the intermediary role of the platform.
2   The platform itself cannot provide guarantees to those who use the platform to invest.
3   The platform cannot create "fund pools."
4   Platforms cannot illegally raise funds from the public.

These basic red lines were then followed by a more extensive set of 10 principles laid out by another CBRC division on 7 September 2014 at the China Internet Financial Innovation and Development Forum. Wang Yanxiu of the CBRC's Banking Innovation Supervision Department laid out the following 10 principles for the industry:

1 Platforms cannot possess investor funds or establish fund pools.
2 Real-name registration for users is required.
3 Platforms are information intermediaries only.
4 The field needs thresholds for entry.
5 Third parties should handle the funds and be audited.
6 Platforms should not supply guarantees.
7 Clarify the fee mechanisms and avoid seeking only projects with high interest rates.
8 Disclose comprehensive information.
9 Reinforce self-regulation.
10 Focus on small loans.

The publication of the "Guiding Opinions" on 18 July 2015 marked the most important day for Chinese P2P regulation so far. The previous speeches gave insight into the CBRC's deliberations on P2P, but the future of the P2P industry depends more on the thinking of China's top leaders. The Opinions received direct approval from China's powerful cabinet, the State Council, and the Communist Party's Central Committee, which is composed of ministers and other elite party members.[8] They provide a window into the framework that resulted from internal debate at the highest levels on how to approach the thorny issue of P2P regulation.

While acknowledging "hidden risks" in Internet finance, the regulators note positively that it has "improved the allocation of capital and advanced innovation." They outline goals for regulation that focus mostly on disclosure, consumer protection, and the generally healthy development of China's financial system and economy. Internet finance should "serve the real economy well." In section 2, they state that regulation will be "moderately loose" overall. Though this statement is vague, it is still a significant signal that the government will leave room for innovation and further development. The document separates "Internet finance" into six categories:

1 Online Payments
2 Online Lending
3 Online Equity Crowdfunding
4 Online Trust
5 Online Insurance
6 Online Fund Sales.

P2P is mostly contained in number 2. The Opinions are too lengthy to analyze their entirety in depth, so the author will focus on the online lending portion as well as significant points from other sections that will have an influence on P2P. Interestingly, the section on Internet lending (section 2, subsection 8) has the only non-Chinese letters in the entire document, used to explicitly state that the following principles apply to P2P. Online lending is defined as "direct lending between individuals realized over Internet platforms." These activities legally fall under the relevant interpersonal lending laws and associated decisions by the Supreme People's Court. The role of these platforms is to facilitate borrowers' and lenders' exchange of information as middlemen and perform credit evaluation. They must clarify their nature as "information intermediaries." They are not to provide credit enhancement or illegally raise funds. Small loan companies should "strive to reduce clients' financing costs." The paragraph ends by assigning regulatory responsibilities to the CRBC. While these statements mostly echo those made previously by CBRC officials, these principles effectively preclude much of the existing P2P system in China, which has been based on guarantees.

While most of the document is relatively uncontroversial, section 3 on a "Solid Institutional System, Regulated Internet Finance Market Order" enforced a change far more radical than most observers expected. In one sentence, the government effectively put P2P under the direct regulation of the banks. Online lenders "should select a financial institution in the banking industry as account custodian, [to] manage and oversee client funds."[9] The accounts must be audited by an independent third party, whose results are shared with clients, and the banks must separate client funds from those of the platform. This section of the regulations is the purview of the PBoC. The effect on P2P is to add two layers of regulation (PBoC and the banks) to that already mentioned from the CBRC.

The departure from previous statements from the CBRC is that this effectively shuts out third party payments operators from performing the account management functions for P2P. Platforms now have no choice but to migrate from the more nimble (and pliable) third party payments companies to China's powerful, conservative banking sector. At the time of this writing, few banks provide such custodian services. Another potential outcome is that the existing third party payments providers collaborate with banks to provide these services, with the payments provider doing most of the service provision and the bank ensuring regulatory compliance.

Until the specifics emerge, including a timeline for implementation, the effect on the industry may be muted. However, it implies a coming revolutionary shift in power from P2P back to the banking system it has been trying to disrupt. The survival of any P2P platform will be at the mercy of banks with very different risk considerations. Market entry will slow as a bottleneck develops around banks that may decide that the risks of handling accounts for a small platform are not worth the potential fees. The extra costs will also be significant. Banks will incur costs to evaluate the risk management processes of platforms, and their custodial/payments services are likely to be much higher than those of the third parties currently doing this business. New Internet-based banks like those backed by Alibaba and Tencent have an opportunity to use their banking licenses for a strong entry into this market. The data and experience that handling these functions gives to the banks means they will pose a much greater threat to the competitiveness of P2P platforms, as they will have direct access to the platforms' client base as well as knowledge of defaults. They may even use this data to push out the platform and run the business themselves.

Knowing the general framework for regulation is helpful for predicting the future direction of regulation, but there is still a great deal of uncertainty about the strictness and interpretation of these principles. In the following section, the author outlines some of these areas and their significance.

One issue that remains to be resolved is the currently widespread model of pre-paying investors when borrowers are behind on payments. Platforms using either platform funds or a loss reserve may violate the CBRC's previous guidance on fund pools and the "information intermediary" requirement, though the platforms would claim otherwise. It also poses risks to platform solvency in the event that a large borrower goes under. The CBRC will need to clarify the definition of "fund pool" to provide clearer guidance and eliminate abuses.

Thresholds for entry also remain unclear, partially because of the difficulty in determining fitting criteria. Most of the existing players started small, so thresholds based on volume and registered capital would have precluded many from entering the industry. Setting the criteria too high would create an undesired reduction in competition by putting up a barrier to entry, which benefits incumbents who have reached large volumes and already. Only companies flush with capital would then be able to become new entrants, such as many listed companies. However, barriers to entry could be the key to reducing the hundreds of cases of frauds in which platform managers "run off" with funds from those who invested on their platforms. The CBRC could create minimum standards for the security of IT architecture, management experience in relevant fields, and equity capital to ensure that industry participants have the expertise and resources necessary to be trusted with directing investor funds through their platforms. The sheer number of industry participants would make enforcement of any standards a time-consuming task, but the CBRC should be given the resources necessary to complete it.

Guarantees have been much debated since the industry took off, and the prohibition on platforms directly offering guarantees is especially relevant to companies like Lufax, which uses a guarantee company also part of the Ping An group. The promises of safety in platform marketing materials and websites (for example, many platforms guarantee principal and interest, and even more guarantee at least investor principal) would seem to imply a guarantee. Platforms claim that only third parties and loan loss reserves (if applicable) are the only resources backing these guarantees, and that they are not legally liable to step in with platform capital for investors if one or both of these proves insufficient. For this principle to become effective regulation, the CBRC needs to make a clear formula for what constitutes a guarantee, including limits on marketing claims by platforms that would violate regulations issued in 2014 and 2015 for wealth management products. It should encourage companies to reduce their reliance on guarantees, which would then help improve investors' ability to differentiate risk.

It must also establish standards for the relationship between platforms and their guarantee companies to ensure that, for example, the guarantees are not made through a company connected with the platform owners. Such connections could create a dangerous conflict of interest. China also needs clear-cut procedures for what happens to loans if the guarantee company fails. The platforms should in this case not be able to step in with their own capital to reimburse loans backed by the now-defunct guarantor. If they did so, they would set a dangerous precedent that would invalidate any claims that they function as only informational intermediaries.

Clarifications of these relationships and disclosure of the guarantee company's financial health are especially important for Chinese P2P because of the prevalence of retail investors. Retail investors are rarely equipped to evaluate the financial health of guarantee companies backing their loans on their own, and it is misleading to create a perception that carrying a guarantee makes the loans risk free. Unlike the US, China has yet to experience a major round of defaults or economic downturn since these guarantee companies were established. A large round of defaults, even concentrated in one region, could bring down enough guarantee companies that work with P2P platforms and shake investor confidence just as investors lost confidence in formerly triple-A rated subprime mortgage securities in the financial crisis. This, however, is a worst-case scenario that can be avoided through effective regulation, extensive disclosure, and continued efforts to educate investors about the risks of P2P, risks that justify the high returns they earn in good times.

As for fees, the CBRC should create standardized disclosure forms for fees. One for investors should clearly indicate the interest rate spread, origination fees, servicing fees, transfer fees (if applicable), and any other applicable costs that may be incurred by the investor. For borrowers, platforms should disclose a total annual percentage rate that shows the total cost of the loan if paid on time, which includes any fees and interest. The standardization would allow regulators and/or third parties to make meaningful comparisons that help investors and borrowers find the best fitting products. It would also award more efficient platforms that charge lower fees.

Of all the debates around regulation, disclosure may be the most important. Transparency in investing and platform management is a key factor differentiating P2P from banks. It is fundamental to equipping investors to make their own properly informed decisions of which platforms to choose and which loans on a given platform they decide to fund. Although platforms voluntarily disclose a great deal of information in order to reassure borrowers and investors they are making a well-informed decision, the lack of standards and required disclosure means it is difficult to analyze and draw meaningful comparisons both between platforms and about the industry as a whole.

For example, platforms are eager to report their total loan volume, which implies that they are a leading company. However, they do not tend to report their average outstanding loans, resulting in overcounting.[10] Platform executives explained to the author that they wanted to prevent calculations of "leverage ratios" based on loans to P2P capital, though leverage should be irrelevant if they are sticking to informational intermediary status and not risking their own capital. Conversely, they are not obligated to report any to the third parties who estimate the total industry size, let alone accurate information, meaning our estimates may also be overstated. Smaller platforms concentrated in a provincial city may have upward of 100 million RMB in loans and still not be counted in data from Online Lending House, leaving a long "tail" of P2P invisible to national authorities and industry analysts. A compulsory disclosure regime for platforms would allow much more accurate analyses of the industry and its risks.

The Opinions tasked the PBoC with the creation of a nationwide P2P industry association that should participate in industry self-regulation. Self-regulation for many oversight functions is sensible when one considers the extent of work required to regulate such a rapidly growing industry with so many players. In fact, industry associations in cities like Beijing and Shanghai are already in place and are performing important functions. For example, platforms requesting to join the association in Shanghai must undergo an audit that verifies the accuracy of the amounts they claim to intermediate. They also must publish their reserves and place them in banks. These are good first steps, but self-regulation should also include certification procedures to help investors avoid platforms with ineffective risk management, insufficient capital to keep the platform running, or outright fraud.

Self-regulation should also include mandatory information sharing on loans across China, not only within individual cities. At the present, insufficient information sharing and the fact that P2P platforms cannot report to the central bank's credit rating system mean that defaults on one platform may not necessarily reflect poorly on an individual or business' creditworthiness indicators. This leaves the platforms and other financial institutions vulnerable to fraud. Borrowers in financial distress may also take out new loans on another of the 2,000 platforms to pay back the others in a dangerous game of "hot potato," making defaults appear lower than they ultimately will turn out to be. Fraudsters may simultaneously take out small denomination loans from numerous platforms to amass loans in the hundreds of thousands or more RMB, but the cost of tracking them down discourages any individual platform from vigorous pursuit in collections. Although there are "black lists" of fraudulent borrowers, real-time, comprehensive information sharing is necessary to ensure the continued healthy development of P2P lending in China. The Opinions' mandate to establish a nationwide Internet lending industry association is an excellent start, but dealing with the thorny issue of its authority and management, especially for sensitive default data, will be a long, drawn out process.

A focus on "small loans" has been much more controversial, coming out originally in CBRC speeches but then not making it into the Opinions. The Opinions mentions both Internet lending and Internet small loans, therefore implying the permission of larger volume Internet lending.

However, exposure should be capped to ensure that any platform does not have excessively concentrated risk in one firm or group of firms. To avoid conflicts of interest, platforms should not be created to funnel money into one company, and excessive concentration goes against the spirit of P2P, a spirit that facilitates decentralization and diversification. However, caps should not be used to shield banks and other large lenders from competition. One P2P executive told the author, "Regulation should not force us to make small loans just for the sake of being small." The goal should be to permit P2P to lend reasonable amounts to companies in the lower end of "S" to the upper end of the "M" in SME, but only if they are large enough to continue operation in the event of default.

The Opinions, while a good start, need the force of law and accompanying penalties for non-compliance. Servicing and platform resolution are two more areas that future regulation must address. Some industry participants predict 90% or so of the firms currently operating will fail in the coming years, especially after the industry is regulated.[11] While nowhere near as difficult to deal with as bank failures, regulators must be prepared to deal with platform bankruptcies. In conversations with regulators, scholars, and industry participants, none was able to provide the author with a clear answer as to who would be responsible for servicing the loans going forward. The CBRC's upcoming regulations should make clarification of the loan servicing arrangement and fees a priority. With clear responsibilities and fees, it will be much easier to, for example, transfer those servicing rights to another entity and avoid a disruption of payments for borrowers who are able to continue payment. Platform resolution would then be much simpler as well.

Regulators should ensure maximum effort is made to ensure loans made by defunct platforms remain to be serviced. If not, it may be difficult to assert later that when it comes to systemic risk, such platforms are not just unregulated banks. Failure of the P2P information intermediary should not mean a disruption in all the credit it helped arrange. If the industry undergoes a major round of consolidation without massive losses to those who invested over the platforms, then P2P will continue to gain acceptance among the Chinese public and government. This confidence can then become the foundation for aggregate growth even more rapid than the present for the remaining platforms and continued encouragement by regulators.

Comparison of regulatory regimes

The three countries outlined here share the characteristic of being the largest markets for P2P. While their regulatory approaches for the sector vary widely, there is significant overlap when it comes to specific measures. This is clear when we examine how P2P fits with the pre-existing regulatory frameworks in each country and then how the regulatory system has responded to its growth.

P2P in the US and UK had to deal with a strict regulatory system that required expensive workarounds to adapt their businesses to it. Indeed, the SEC almost shut down the leading US players in the early stages because of the novelty of the securities backed by consumer loans that they tried to register. The firms need to comply with regulation meant for banks (for loan issuance), securities companies (for disclosure and issuance of securitizations), and many other types of entity depending on state-level regulations. The UK, on the other hand, lumped them in with other consumer finance companies until 2014.

By contrast, China is now by far the largest market, partially because the existing regulatory system left a large vacuum with low barriers to entry and compliance costs. They were able to use a well-developed legal structure around interpersonal lending, a lack of national rules for their sector, and the impossibility of local jurisdictions to handle these nationwide businesses to create the room they needed to grow with astonishing rapidity. One could register a business, set up a website, and begin collecting investor funds from all around China without spending the millions of dollars and many years of work with each state authority and multiple federal ones it would take for a US company.

Now that things are changing, there are remarkable similarities in how each country is altering its regulatory approach. The UK and China have placed responsibility for regulation in the hands of one regulator, the FCA and the CBRC, respectively. The US, however, has not changed its regulatory structure, leaving the new players to deal with a multitude of regulators at multiple levels. With respect to innovation, the FCA in the UK and the Consumer Financial Protection Bureau (CFPB) in the US have both established special programs (Innovation Hub in the former, Project Catalyst in the latter) to create a less formal, more frequent dialogue between regulator and regulated in this space to reduce uncertainty in how regulation will be applied to new business models. The CBRC has put P2P regulation in its financial inclusion office, giving a clear signal that it sees P2P's potential to cover people whose needs are unmet by the existing financial system.

Many aspects of the specific requirements the UK system applies to P2P companies are in the proposed CBRC rules, such as qualifications for management, balanced advertisements, bans on self-guaranteeing loans, and segregation of client funds. The State Council and the CBRC have made it clear that these platforms should be "information intermediaries" rather than "credit intermediaries." Aspects of the business that used to be done by one firm now must be separate, with loan issuance and custodian services for client funds undertaken by firms in the banking industry. This measure will lead Chinese P2P to converge to what is already the norm in the US, where banks like WebBank issue loans, and UK, where client funds must be held in segregated bank accounts.

Notes

1 "Differences between the Scope of the OFT and FCA Regimes." *Financial Conduct Authority*. 14 August 2015. https://www.the-fca.org.uk/differences-between-scope-oft-and-fca-regimes?field_fcasf_sector=226&field_fcasf_page_category=unset Accessed 27 March 2016.
2 Ibid.
3 "Project Innovate: Next Steps." *Financial Conduct Authority*. 2016. https://innovate.fca.org.uk/innovation-hub/summary-rules-loan-based-crowdfunding-platforms Accessed 26 March 2016.
4 "Regulatory Sandbox." *Financial Conduct Authority*. November 2015. https://www.fca.org.uk/static/documents/regulatory-sandbox.pdf Accessed 26 March 2016.
5 "Summary of Rules for Loan-Based Crowdfunding Platforms." *Financial Conduct Authority*. 2016. https://innovate.fca.org.uk/innovation-hub/summary-rules-loan-based-crowdfunding-platforms Accessed 27 March 2016.

6 "Peer-to-Peer Finance Association Operating Principles." *P2PFA*. http://p2pfa.info/wp-content/uploads/2015/09/Operating-Principals-vfinal.pdf Accessed 27 March 2016.
7 The PBoC estimated shadow banking's (entrusted loans, trust loans, and undiscounted bankers' acceptances) contribution to total social financing at 18% in 2014. People's Bank of China News. 29 January 2015. http://www.pbc.gov.cn/publish/english/955/2015/20150129085803713420369/20150129085803713420369_.html Accessed 27 March 2016.
8 "Regulatory Agencies Publish 'Guiding Opinions' on Advancing the Healthy Development of Internet Finance." 18 July 2015. http://www.cbrc.gov.cn/chinese/home/docDOC_ReadView/DD36A6654C7E4D0D9D658E712B-FB46C5.html Accessed 27 March 2016.
9 "Guiding Opinions" section 3, subsection 14.
10 Just under 60% of P2P loans mature one to three months after issuance, so any repeat borrowers of these maturities who roll over their loans would be counted 4–12 times in one year for total issuance. The average amount outstanding, however, would be lower.
11 "CBRC States P2P Cannot Provide Guarantees: Industry Insider: 90% of P2P Will Fail." *Xinhua News*. 9 July 2014. http://news.xinhuanet.com/fortune/2014–07/09/c_126728849.htm Accessed 30 June 2015.

5 Outlook for P2P in China

P2P has incredible potential to remake the way finance is done in China if it is done right. As the Internet reaches more of the population, accumulated data on consumers and businesses improve risk modeling, regulation helps control risks, and the platforms themselves improve, Chinese households and businesses will find themselves with many more attractive choices for investment and borrowing. That is not to say that this is right around the corner or that the route is not fraught with risk. The market today is untested by economic downturns, regulatory compliance, and large scandals. In fact, there is a consensus among experts the author interviewed for this report that the majority of platforms are likely to fail in the coming years, especially with coming regulation that will challenge many currently profitable business models and reduce regulatory arbitrage.

Short term

In the short term, P2P faces many challenges. The nascent industry must earn the confidence of the public and government through the coming industry consolidation, which some predict will lead to bankruptcy of over half to 90% of today's platforms. Those who cannot compete or comply with coming regulation must exit the market in an orderly fashion and make efforts to ensure the loans they intermediated remain serviced.

Another challenge is to retain this trust while gradually reducing the role of guarantees. While platforms may be right that guarantees and the appearance of unvarying returns is important at this stage to get investors familiar with P2P, the industry should shift the risk to investors over the medium term. It is dangerous to create the illusion that P2P returns are "guaranteed," especially considering the aforementioned gaps in credit data and short history of both P2P and guarantee companies. Investors in Lending Club's platform see widely varying returns based on their portfolio, but it has still grown impressively. Sufficient diversification, not guarantees, should reduce volatility for investors. P2P would then be part of showing investors that fixed income instruments are not riskless but can still provide strong returns. In any case, coming regulation may prohibit some of the guarantee and pre-payment practices prevalent in the industry, so firms should prepare for this possibility.

The initial round of regulations will set off the first round of industry consolidation. It will put poorly run, uncompetitive firms out of business and demonstrate the ability of those who remain to stay competitive despite higher compliance costs. Most important, the barriers to entry will make setting up a fraudulent platform to run off with client money more difficult. Compulsory disclosures will shed light on the true size and risk of the industry, especially non-performing loans.

Dominant e-commerce companies will leverage their advantages in data, name recognition, and distribution channels to enter the market, challenging the fledgling smaller and medium-sized platforms. Alibaba's Zhaocai Bao platform created a 14 billion RMB marketplace in its first six months of operation alone and has set a goal to transact P2P loans of 163 billion USD by the end of 2016.[1]

Another trend we will see in the short term is more collaboration between different types of firms. The Guiding Opinions directly encouraged online lenders and existing financial institutions to work together, bringing the advantages of each into mutually beneficial partnerships. For example, the requirement to have banks as custodians for client funds could lead third party payments operators who currently work with P2P to offer products to clients together with banks, complying with regulation, ensuring safety for client funds, and continuing to add product innovation through technology. Other models will arise, such as Dianrong's partnership with banks to help them build their own P2P platforms and provide more user-friendly ways to manage their capital and client relationships.

Medium and long term

Beyond the short term, when it has a firmly established record of reliability, effective credit rating, solid regulatory compliance, and cost advantage versus other players due to its embrace of technology, P2P's outlook looks very bright. Consolidation and higher barriers to entry in the future may pare down the number of platforms significantly from today's around 2,000, but the market could continue to support hundreds of thriving platforms, from all-around service providers with their own asset exchanges to niche players with an advantage intermediating loans in specific industries.

Although China may not see days of 10% real economic growth again in the near future, the potential size of the market from an increased focus on domestic consumption and continued entrepreneurial activity will drive continued growth in the SME loan market. This is P2P's sweet spot, and it could far outpace growth in the broader economy.

Gradual opening of China's financial markets to foreign investment and relaxation of restrictions on who can lend also present a medium-term opportunity for P2P. If the low yield environment continues, foreign institutional investors will jump at the opportunity to gain reliable, high returns by investing over P2P platforms, just as US-based venture capital firms have been among the primary investors in Chinese P2P platforms whose total VC investment take in 2014 was 15.5 billion USD according to the Strontium Group.[2] The rise in supply of funds would then reduce funding costs for enterprises and help alleviate the much maligned "difficult and expensive financing" for SMEs and consumers in China. It would also contribute to the internationalization of the RMB as foreign institutional investors flocked into these high-yielding RMB-denominated assets.

Though it may seem unlikely at the present, the author believes that some of the leading P2P companies will become banks in the long run, and banks will also begin to look more like P2P companies. Approval to become banks may not be as far off as it may appear. Companies like Alibaba and Tencent have already been approved to set up banks in a new pilot program to open up the banking sector to private banks. Although it will take time, successful operation of these banks will encourage the government to continue to expand the program. Regulation that increases compliance costs for P2P companies like CreditEase, with offline branches across China and a wide variety of wealth management services beyond its P2P platform Yirendai, may decide to take this step so they can take in deposits and participate in the official credit rating system.

Notes

1 Smith, Tharon and Lew, Christopher, 2015. "Peer-to-Peer Lending in China: Investment Environment." Strontium Group.
2 Ibid.

Conclusion

P2P in China encompasses a wide variety of financial and informational intermediaries, from pawnshops and small loan companies banding together online to asset exchanges run by one of China's most respected financial institutions. For now, firms number in the thousands and loans intermediated are in the tens of billions of US dollars. Development at this pace does not come by chance. P2P has fit perfectly into cultural predilections for lending between individuals, and technological progress allows it to leverage the Internet to both reach more people and eventually cut costs of providing financial services. Supportive government policies and an economic environment ripe for new ways to borrow and invest played key roles as well for the demand side, the supply side, and the flexibility to satisfy those needs.

Just as in any new industry, but especially for finance, there are growing pains. Hundreds of platforms have already failed, and hundreds more may collapse in the coming years as regulation, stiffer competition, and slower economic growth challenge their business models. While the failure of smaller players will probably help funds flow to larger players, the failure of a large platform due to excessive "pre-payments" for late borrowers out of its own capital, stepping in for a failed guarantee company to back the loans, exhaustion of its loan loss reserves, or some other unforeseen factor could be much more damaging to the industry's image. It would be all the more severe if no arrangements were made for continuing to service the loans, leaving investors on their own with the impracticable task of collecting on the small fraction of loans they own. To reduce this risk, P2P will need to focus more on the pure informational intermediary role and allow investors to absorb the risk.

Regulation should focus on a rigorous, standardized disclosure regime that includes bad/overdue loans and effective oversight of companies, whether they call themselves P2P or not, matching borrowers and lenders. Sufficient resources must be devoted to verifying this disclosure and presenting it in a way that allows investors and borrowers to find the most fitting option. Rules should allow continued experimentation in business models while protecting investors as well as maintaining overall financial and economic stability. As P2P gets larger, getting these rules right will only increase in importance. Chinese P2P differs from that in other markets in the scale it has achieved in a remarkably short period and the freedom it has had from regulatory restrictions. While this lack of regulation is about to end, the government's consistent support means the specific regulations to come are unlikely to be too restrictive for P2P to continue its development.

Despite these challenges in operation and regulation, P2P has a bright future in China. The underlying factors behind its rise are not going anywhere. It has the potential to provide a much-needed liberalization of China's financial sector with market-based interest rates for borrowers and investors, directing capital to areas of China's economy previously spurned by big banks like small businesses and consumer credit. While the costs remain high for P2P today for customer acquisition, credit rating, and collections, technological developments and accumulation of data will increase its competitiveness. More established financial institutions with legacy costs and less ability to adapt will lose market share if they do not keep up. Today's P2P players are already exploring private bank licensing and forays into wealth management businesses. Banks are slowly opening up their own P2P platforms, sometimes with the help of current platforms. Thus, activities performed by different types of financial institutions will converge even as business models diverge and become more specialized. It is important to note that these trends are not unique to China. They will challenge the existing regulatory models around the world.

China has learned and continued to learn from the West from the beginning of its Reform and Opening Up in 1978, but tables have been turning since the subprime and Euro crises. Its regulation specifically designed for P2P will emerge and likely serve as a reference for P2P regulation that eventually emerges in the US and elsewhere. Its companies may create a set of best practices that it exports abroad through expansions and eventual IPOs in the US. When it comes to P2P, the rest of the world may well soon be learning from China.

Note

This report was completed in August 2015. Since then, the P2P industry in China has undergone significant changes. With regulations pending, problems began to emerge along with rapid development, and platforms that engaged in illegal fundraising were banned according to the law. Some others experienced operational difficulty. The number of problem platforms reached 896 in 2015, 3.26 times of that in the previous year. The CBRC, together with other supervisory authorities, issued a draft regulation on the P2P industry for consultation at the end of 2015. But the formal regulation had not been published at the time this report went to press (September 2016). Instead, China launched a crackdown on misconduct, especially illegal fundraising in Internet finance. The P2P industry is an area of special focus. As a result, how China's P2P industry will develop in the future remains to be seen.

Appendix

Assessment report of online P2P lending platforms in China 2015

Foreword

To promote the healthy development of the P2P industry, to provide an authoritative, detailed assessment report on the development of this industry, and to provide some fundamental data and references for regulators, the SFI Center for Internet Finance Research P2P Research Group has conducted research on the development of P2P platform development and risk management to produce the "Assessment Report of Online P2P Lending Platforms in China." This research was conducted with academic support of the CF40 and CFCITY.

There are multiple reports on the market regarding P2P market development, assessment, and ratings. This survey has its own unique characteristics in the following aspects. First, the 19 P2P platforms that participated in the survey provided fairly comprehensive data describing their operations, related not only just to the development of their platforms, but also to the structure of their equity stakeholders and company governance. Only with this information available was it possible to evaluate the platforms' development and risks. Second, the sample used is very representative, including large platforms as well as platforms that have been operational only for six months; it includes platforms that operate online only, as well as platforms that function both online and offline.

The following conclusions have been reached from this survey.

First, P2P platforms have expanded very rapidly, with registered capital, offline presence, number of managers and employees, and scale of loan activity all expanding many times over each year.

Second, some P2P platforms are already more than just a simple information intermediary. Although P2P platforms define themselves as information intermediaries, a great many platforms also have protection mechanism for lenders when borrowers default, such as risk reserve funds and loan guarantee, with some platforms even entering into capital transactions and becoming to some degree a kind of credit intermediary.

Third, there are big differences among P2P platforms in their business models: some platforms continue to operate online only, while others operate both online and offline; some platforms' revenue mainly relies on account maintenance fees, while others have taken steps to diversify their sources of income; some platforms continue with micro credit lending, while others are primarily engaged in collateral loans, and some cooperate with a third party partner; some platforms only function in one region, while others operate across the whole country.

Fourth, P2P platforms share the characteristic of concentrated risk. From the survey it is apparent that many P2P platforms have very concentrated loans. Given that so many P2P platforms in reality have to some degree already become credit intermediaries, the high concentration of loans indicates a high concentration of risks. In the event of large loss from a single loan, there is the possibility that a P2P platform's risk reserve funds or even net capital could be entirely wiped out.

Synthesizing the results of this survey, the research group has proposed the following regulatory suggestions.

First, P2P regulators should clarify the nature of the platforms. The survey shows P2P platforms in China could continue as information intermediaries or they could become actual credit intermediaries. For these two different types of platforms with different functions, regulators should enact different sets of rules. For information intermediaries, regulators should require platforms to have adequate information disclosure, but in the case of credit intermediaries, a reference should be made to how banks and financial institutions are regulated, with regulation requirements that are stricter than information intermediaries. There should be no space for regulatory arbitrage for these two different types of platforms.

Second, P2P platforms can use guarantors, but there must be standards. First, P2P platforms themselves and their affiliated parties cannot underwrite their loans. Second, P2P platforms may bring in third party guarantors. Finally, P2P platforms must adequately perform information disclosure.

Third, P2P platform lending should be less concentrated. P2P platforms, both information intermediaries and credit intermediaries, could be threatened by highly concentrated lending practices. Possible solutions for regulating the concentration of loans include setting an upper limit for the size of a single loan or setting the maximum ratio of a single loan to the platform's net capital, as can be referred to the 10% cap of bank loans. Different information disclosure standards could be set up for loans of different sizes, with large loans requiring more stringent standards for information disclosure.

Fourth, P2P platforms fund custodianship must be put in place. To protect against all types of fraud, P2P platforms should set up third party fund custody, but there should be a system to guarantee that the third part custody is legitimate and effective. Some platforms use "depository" instead of fund custody, but this is misleading to investors. These platforms place client funds or risk reserve funds in third party institutions like the bank, while still retaining the right to control the funds, which means there actually is no fund custodianship.

Fifth, comprehensive regulations are required to promote the development of a credit reporting system. First, we should permit P2P platforms to link up with the central bank's credit reporting system as quickly as possible. Second, we should promote the development of commercial credit reporting agencies. Finally, self-regulatory organizations should encourage P2P platforms to share their information.

Finally, there should be a unified, standardized system for P2P platform information disclosure. First, high standards for information disclosure should be put in place. Second, P2P platform information disclosure needs to be unified and standardized. A "soft regulation" on P2P platforms' capital adequacy ratio could be instituted through information disclosure.

1 The characteristics and standards of P2P platforms

1.1 P2P platforms' equity ownership structures are highly concentrated, but there is a move toward decentralization

Of the 19 P2P platforms surveyed for this report, 18 chose to disclose information regarding their equity ownership structure. On the basis of the information provided by these 18 platforms, the equity ownership structures of P2P platforms tend to be concentrated. Out of all the single largest stakeholders among all the platforms, the smallest had an equity share larger than 30%, and over 70% of platforms' largest equity shareholders maintained more than 50% ownership. As of Q1 2015, out of the 18 P2P platforms that disclosed information on ownership structures, the largest number of shareholders for any single platform was 9, and most of the platforms had only 3 to 5 shareholders.

However, there is a trend toward the decentralization of P2P platforms' equity ownership. At the beginning of 2014, the average number of shareholders among the 18 P2P platforms was 3.1, but by Q1 2015 the average had increased to 3.7. During this period, 46.7% of platforms saw their number of shareholders increase, 40% stayed the same, while only 13.3% saw a decline in the number of shareholders.

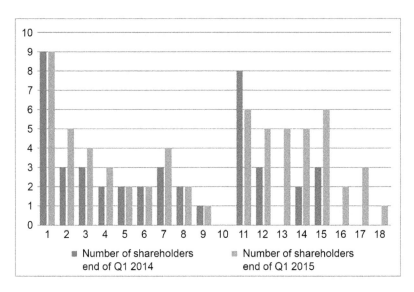

Figure 1 Number of P2P platform shareholders (persons)

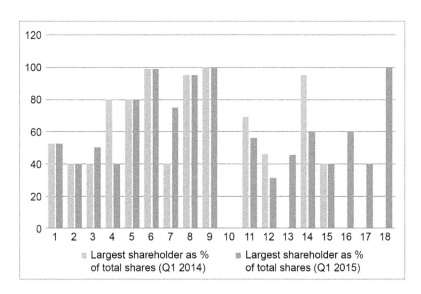

Figure 2 Equity ownership of the largest shareholder (%)

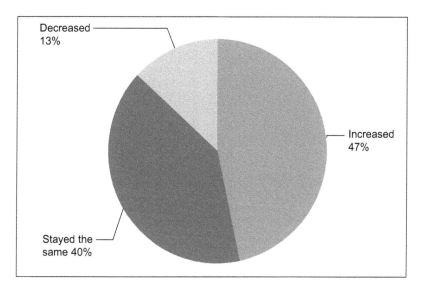

Figure 3 P2P platforms change in the number of shareholders, Q1 2014 to Q1 2015

1.2 The explosive capital growth of P2P platforms

Registered capital is the basis for starting a company. Of the 19 P2P platforms surveyed, 14 platforms in Q1 2015 had registered capital that exceeded 30 million RMB, which is a considerable scale. However, there are some platforms whose registered capital is relatively small in scale.

Since 2014 P2P platforms' registered capital has seen explosive growth. For the platforms that provided complete quarterly data, from Q1 2014 to Q1 2015 over half of these platforms' registered capital had grown by more than 500%.

Because China's registered capital system enforces subscribed capital requirements, paid-in capital is actually more important. This survey shows P2P platforms' registered capital is by-and-large matched by their paid-in capital. In Q1 2015, 72% of platforms' registered capital was roughly consistent with the paid-in capital, while 28% had paid-in capital that was less than the registered capital.

1.3 The governance of P2P platforms has to be improved

As loan information intermediaries, the operations of P2P platforms involve the interests of many of investors. It is for this reason that P2P platforms

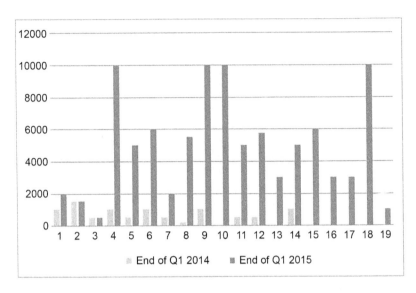

Figure 4 P2P platforms' registered capital (10 thousand RMB)

Note: Some quarterly data is missing because information disclosure is incomplete or the platform was established after 2014.

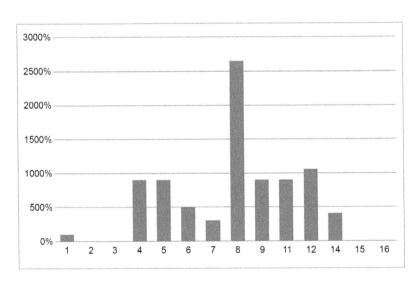

Figure 5 P2P platforms' registered capital growth rate, Q1 2014 to Q1 2015 (%)

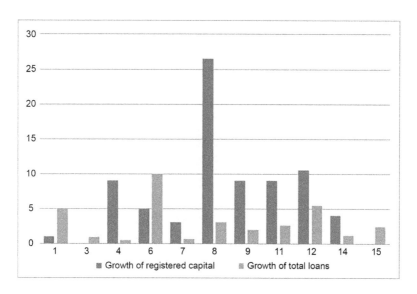

Figure 6 P2P platforms' registered capital growth rate and loan balance growth rate, Q1 2014 to Q1 2015 (%)

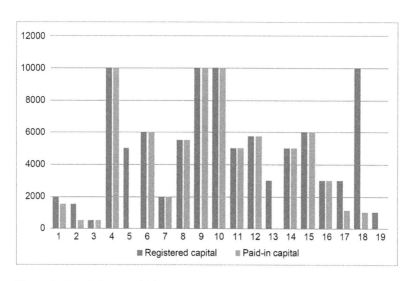

Figure 7 P2P platforms paid-in capital as compared to registered capital at the end of Q1 2015 (10 thousand RMB)

need to improve their company governance. This is necessary to protect the interests of investors and to maintain financial stability. On the basis of this survey, as of the end of Q1 2015, 11 of the 19 platforms included in the survey (58%) established a board of directors, and 8 (42%) established a board of supervisors.

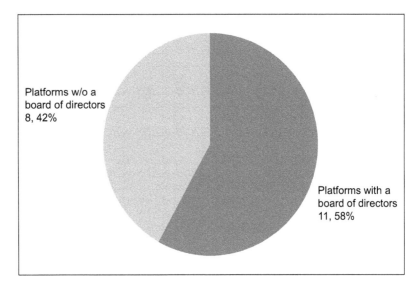

Figure 8 P2P platforms with a board of directors at the end of Q1 2015

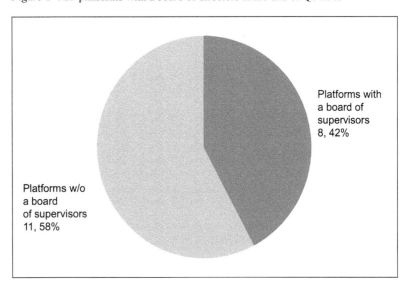

Figure 9 P2P platforms with a board of supervisors at the end of Q1 2015

The decision to establish a board of directors is not clearly related to the length of time a platform has been in operation; for example, at the end of Q1 2015 only 7 of the 12 (58.3%) "early" platforms established before 2013 had boards of directors in place, which is basically in line with the whole sample.

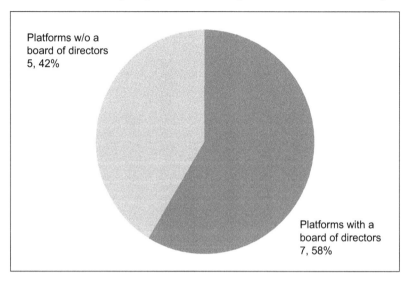

Figure 10 Platforms established before 2013 with a board of directors in place at the end of Q1 2015

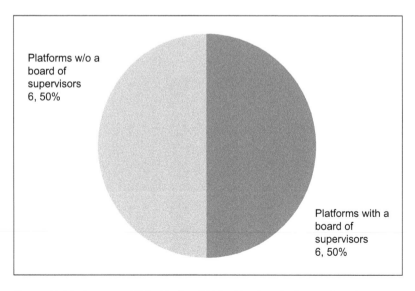

Figure 11 Platforms established before 2013 with a board of supervisors in place at the end of Q1 2015

According to information disclosed by P2P platforms that had either a board of directors or a board of supervisors in place, boards of directors for P2P platforms typically include three to five members, while boards of

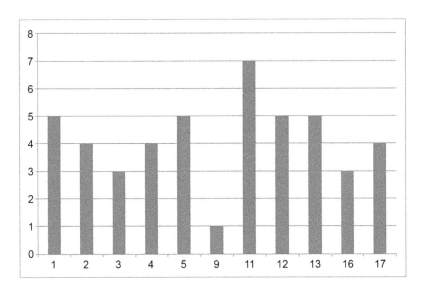

Figure 12 Size of P2P platforms board of directors as of end of Q1 2015 (persons)

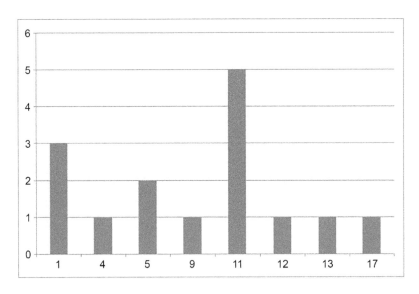

Figure 13 Size of P2P platforms board of supervisors as of end of Q1 2015 (persons)

supervisors usually only include one or two members. The company governance of P2P platforms is still just starting out.

1.4 P2P platform management teams have diverse backgrounds

As startup companies, P2P platforms' management teams are playing an
essential role, and their management style decides the style of the platform overall. As of Q1 2015, the 19 platforms included in this survey had
10 members on their management team on average. Furthermore, most platforms' management teams expanded in size since 2013, with some management teams doubling in size.

P2P platforms' management teams come from diverse backgrounds. As
a typical example of the "Internet +finance" paradigm, P2P managers come
from both traditional financial institutions as well as from Internet and IT
companies.

Of the 17 platforms that disclosed relevant information, by the end of Q1
2015, 15 platforms had more than two managers with work experience at
a traditional financial institution, while 13 had more than three managers
with work experience at a traditional financial institution. By the end of Q1
2015, each platform had on average five managers with work experience at

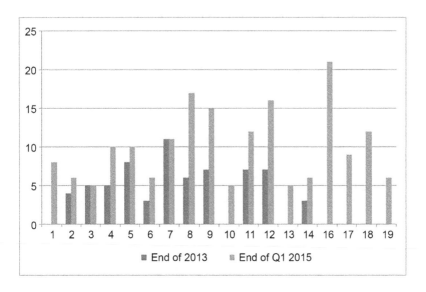

Figure 14 Size of P2P platforms' management teams (persons)

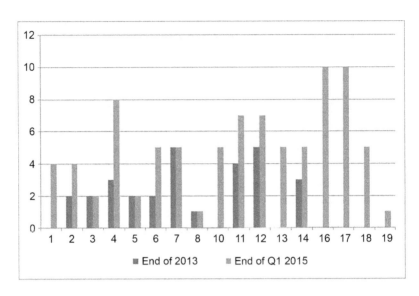

Figure 15 Number of managers with work experience at traditional financial institutions (persons)

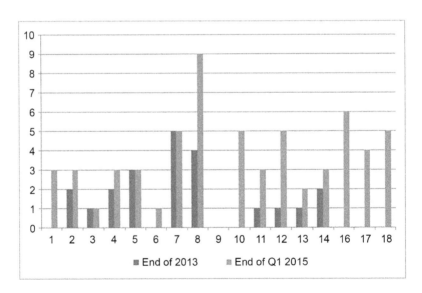

Figure 16 Number of managers with either Internet or IT related work experience (persons)

traditional financial institutions, encompassing about 50% of the management team, consistent with 2013.

Of the 17 platforms that disclosed information, by the end of Q1 2015, 15 platforms reported more than two managers with either Internet or IT experience, with 14 platforms reporting more than three managers with related work experience. By the end of Q1 2015, each platform on average had 3.8 managers with Internet related work experience, constituting approximately 36% of the management team, consistent with 2013.

1.5 The nature of P2P platform determines offline services

P2P platforms are online loan information intermediaries. However, because P2P platforms are not yet connected to the official credit reporting system, and commercial credit reporting systems are underdeveloped, most P2P platforms usually create their own offline services to perform credit-reporting services. Some of the larger platforms have established dozens or even hundreds of offline locations. What's more, since 2014 the scale of offline service sites has expanded rapidly. For the 12 platforms that had information to disclose (the other platforms either came online late or never established offline services), their number of offline sites typically doubled from the end of 2013 to the end of Q1 2015, with some platforms expanding their number of offline sites by more than 10 times.

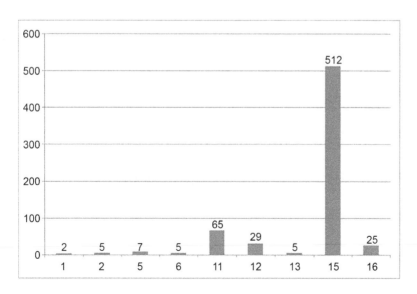

Figure 17 Number of offline service sites for platforms at the end of Q1 2015 (sites)

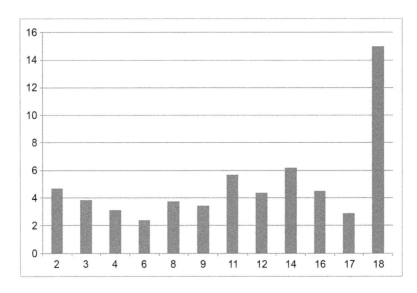

Figure 18 Expansion of offline services (times)

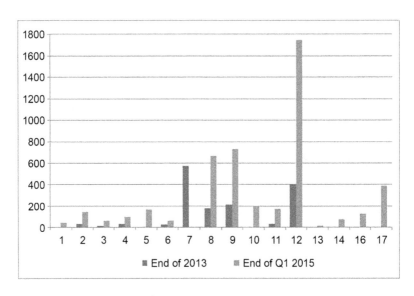

Figure 19 P2P platform employees (persons)

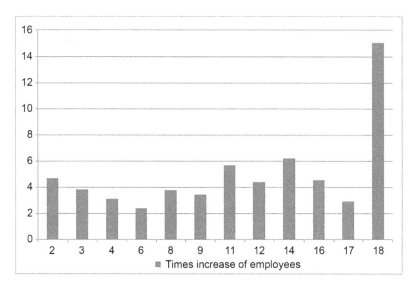

Figure 20 Expansion of P2P platform staff size from end of 2013 to Q1 2015 (times)

1.6 The two extremes of P2P platform staff sizes

Because the P2P platforms have been in operation for varying lengths of time, there is a great difference in P2P platforms' staff size. They tend to be either very large or very small. Some platforms employ between 10 and 20 people only, while other platforms maintain more than 1,000 employees. By comparing the differences between the size of staff for platforms at the end of 2013 and the end of Q1 2015, it becomes apparent that the scale of P2P platforms' staff size has expanded rapidly. On the basis of the survey, since 2013 the P2P platform staff that expanded the slowest still grew by 1.4 times, while the platform with the fastest expanding staff grew by more than 10 times.

1.7 Venture capital is an important source of funding for P2P platforms

Since P2P is an emerging industry, something that has drawn a lot of attention is that many platforms have received funding from VC, PE, or other organizations. For example, out of the 19 platforms that we surveyed, 7 received venture capital funding between 2013 and Q1 2015, 36.8% of the total. Given that some of the platforms surveyed came online rather late, at this stage

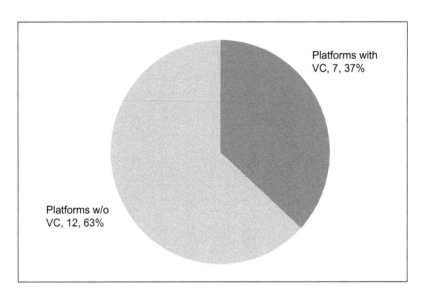

Figure 21 P2P platforms receiving VC funding between 2013 and Q1 2015

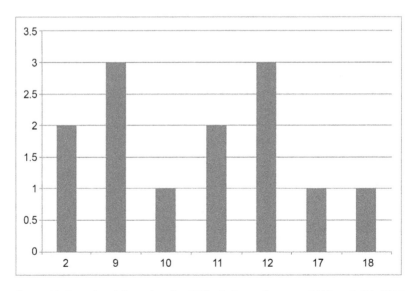

Figure 22 Rounds of financing for P2P platforms between 2013 and Q1 2015 (rounds)

many of them still operate with their own funds, and the percentage of P2P platforms that receive funding could increase even further in the future.

Consecutive funding has become the bright spot of P2P platform financing. As soon as a P2P platform receives its first round of financing, it will often open up its second round of financing soon thereafter. Sometimes, just as the first round of financing is being completed, the next round will have already begun. Out of the eight platforms in this survey that have financing experience, in just two years four of the platforms have already completed two rounds of funding, and two platforms have completed three rounds.

1.8 P2P platforms' assets vary widely in scale, and debt ratios are high

P2P platforms' assets vary widely in scale. As of the end of Q1 2015, the total assets of some small P2P platforms was only 5 million RMB (the assets of the platform itself, not of its clients), and large platforms had assets of more than 800 million RMB. No matter the scale, the total assets of all P2P platforms have expanded rapidly. On the basis of relevant data disclosed by a few platforms, even the slowest expanding platform saw a 20% growth in asset size from the end of 2013 to the end of Q1 2015. Some platforms saw an asset growth of 20 times during this period.

Following data of total assets and liabilities released by the platforms, it is apparent that the asset-liability ratio of P2P platforms is relatively high. For

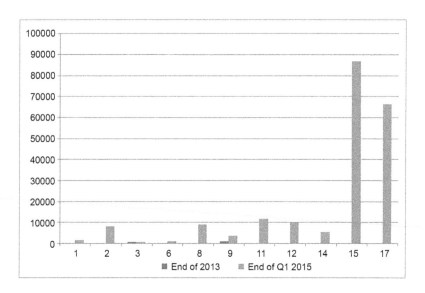

Figure 23 P2P platforms' total assets (10 thousand RMB)

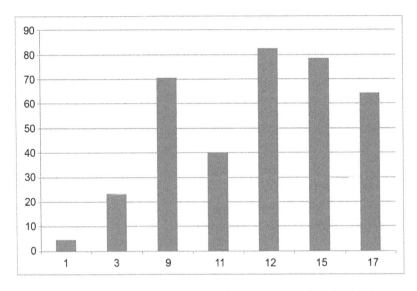

Figure 24 Asset to liability ratio of P2P platforms at the end of Q1 2015 (%)

example, on the basis of data provided by seven platforms, there were four platforms whose asset-liability ratio exceeded 60% at the end of Q1 2015.

2 Overview of P2P operations

2.1 P2P platforms' outstanding loans are growing fast and are highly concentrated

As an emerging industry, P2P business has been growing at an expo-nential rate. The outstanding loans of P2P platforms grew rapidly in 2014, indicating a strong development momentum. For platforms that can provide data for more than one year, almost 80% of them experi-enced over 100% annual growth in loans. By the end of Q1 2015, the total outstanding loans of all platforms were almost 30 billion RMB, with annual growth of 240%.

It has been discussed at length whether or not there should be an upper limit for a single loan on P2P platforms. Some platforms have decided to disclose the loan balance of their single largest lending and the aggregate amount of their top 10 largest loans. The survey shows that almost three tenths of the platforms' single largest loan is more than 10% of total loans, and almost half of the platform's top 10 largest loans in aggregate exceed

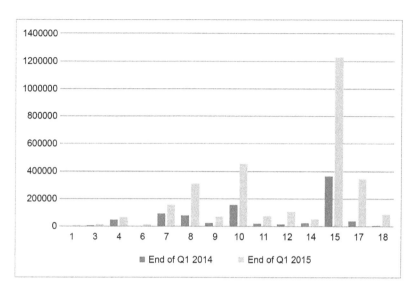

Figure 25 Outstanding loans on P2P platforms (10 thousand RMB)

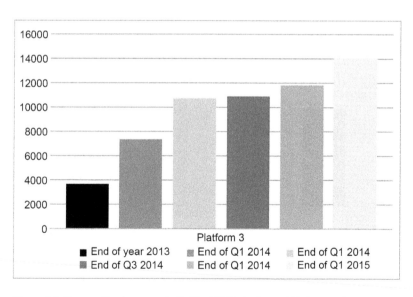

Figure 26 Outstanding loans on individual P2P platforms (10 thousand RMB)

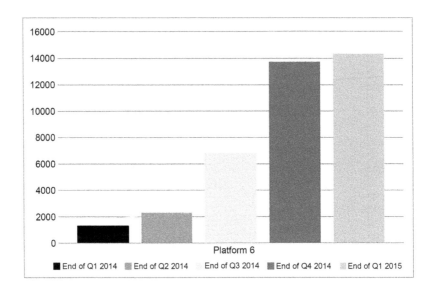

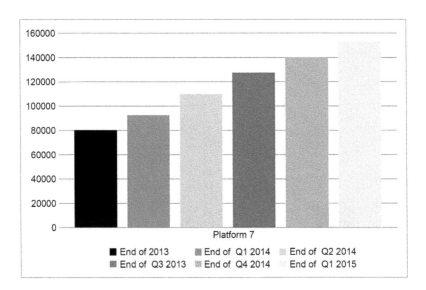

Figure 26 (Continued)

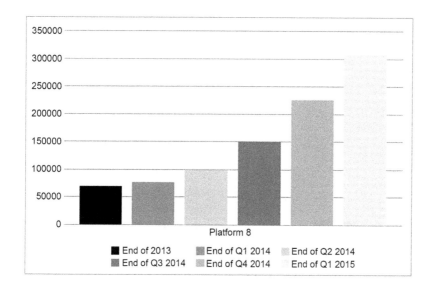

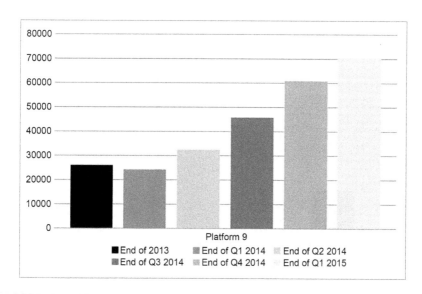

Figure 26 (Continued)

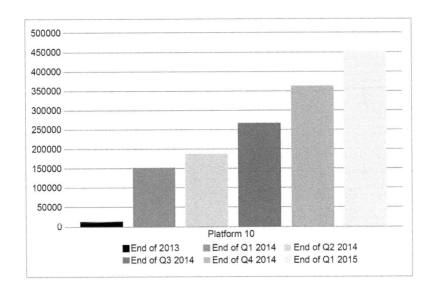

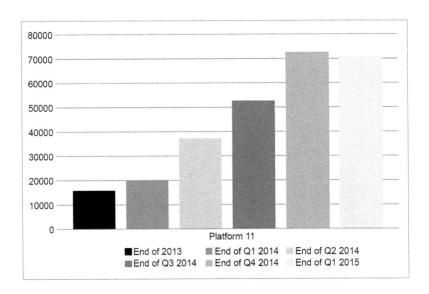

Figure 26 (Continued)

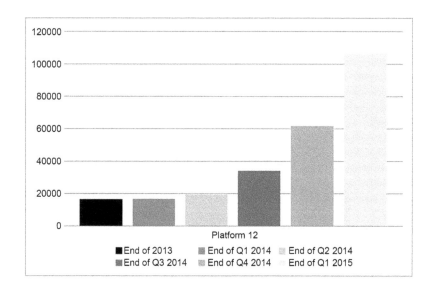

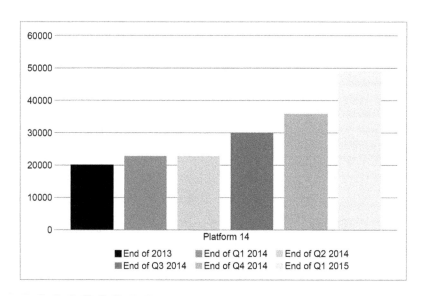

Figure 26 (Continued)

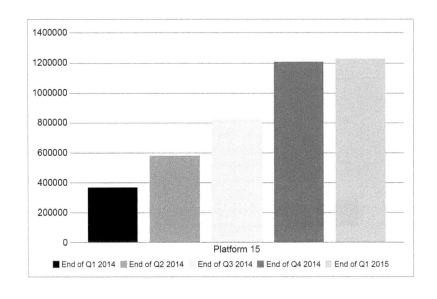

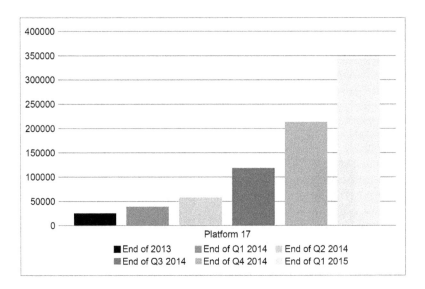

Figure 26 (Continued)

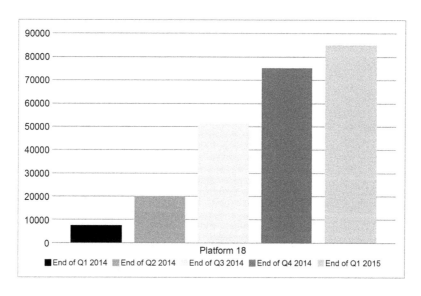

Figure 26 (Continued)

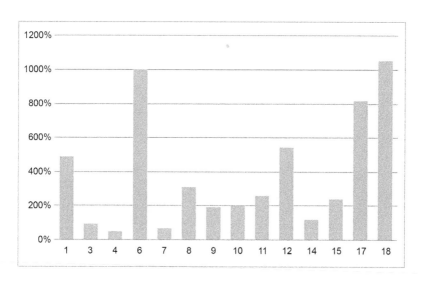

Figure 27 P2P platforms' annual growth of outstanding loans from Q1 2014 to Q1 2015 (%)

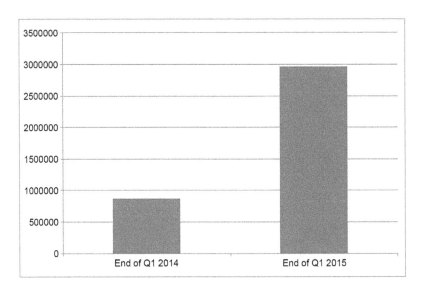

Figure 28 P2P platforms' total outstanding loans (10 thousand RMB)

Note: This figure includes only 14 platforms with data available for Q1 2014 and Q1 2015.

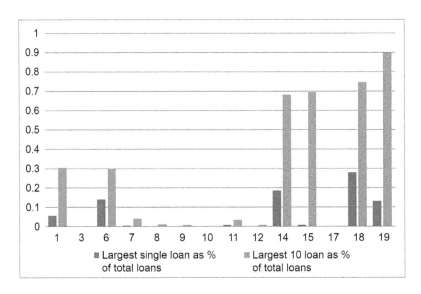

Figure 29 P2P platform loan concentration, Q1 2015 (%)

over 30% of total loans. This illustrates a high concentration of lending for some P2P platforms.

2.2 *P2P platforms show rapid annual growth in new loans*

P2P platforms' annual growth in new loans has also been substantial. On the basis of data provided by platforms for 2013 and 2014, new loans nearly doubled in 2014, growing to 16 billion RMB from 8 billion RMB in 2013. Among these platforms, about half of them saw an annual growth of over 200%.

2.3 *P2P platforms' loan maturities vary but generally become longer*

The maturities of new loans differ greatly among platforms. Some mostly lend out short-term loans, issuing most new loans with maturities of three months or less. There are also some platforms with the vast majority of loans lasting more than 12 months. For platforms whose new loans are mostly concentrated in the long term, their loans also tend to be highly concentrated, with the outstanding loans of the single largest borrower or the aggregate of the top 10 biggest borrowers accounting for a large proportion of the total.

Overall, maturities for P2P platform loans are lengthening. More than half of loans issued in 2013 had duration of three months or less. By 2014 although the total amount of loans with shorter than three-month maturity had increased, their proportion of total lending had declined, while the proportion of loans with durations longer than 12 months had increased.

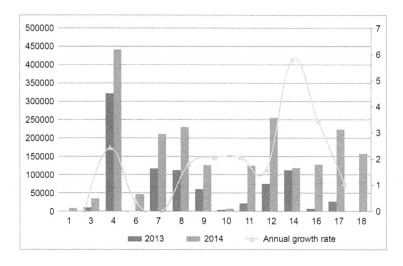

Figure 30 P2P platforms new loans in one year (10 thousand RMB)

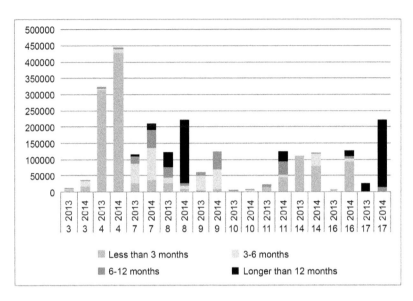

Figure 31 Maturity structure of P2P platforms' new loans (10 thousand RMB)

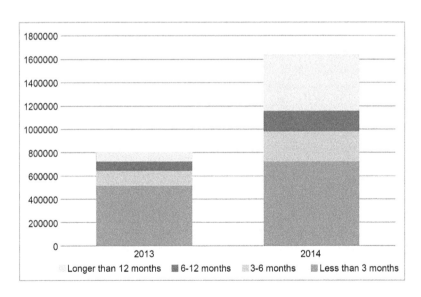

Figure 32 Term structure of new loans (10 thousand RMB)

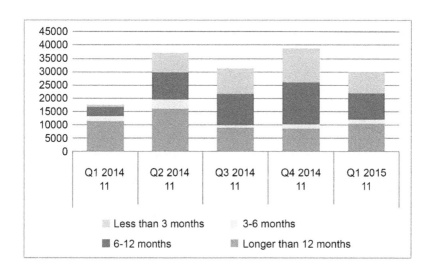

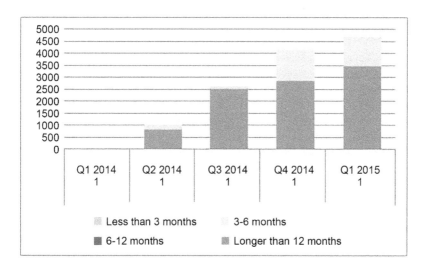

Figure 33 Maturity structure of quarter on quarter new loans for individual P2P platforms (10 thousand RMB)

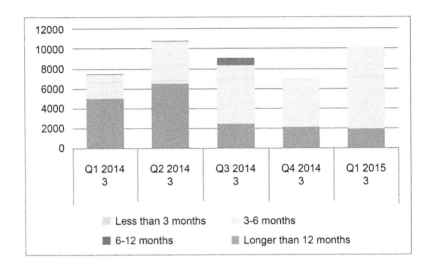

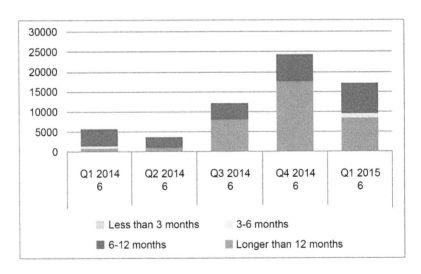

Figure 33 (Continued)

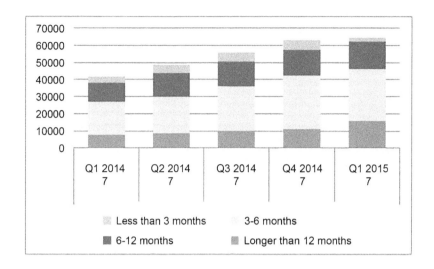

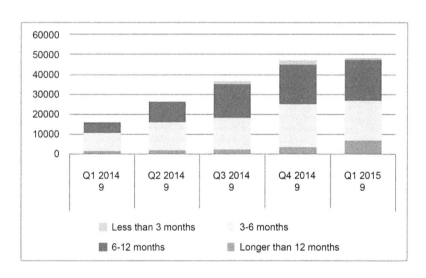

Figure 33 (Continued)

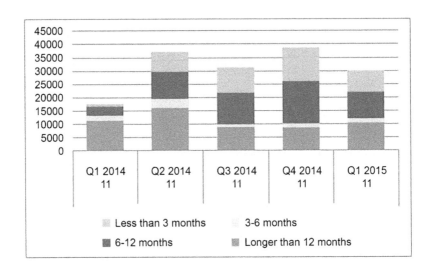

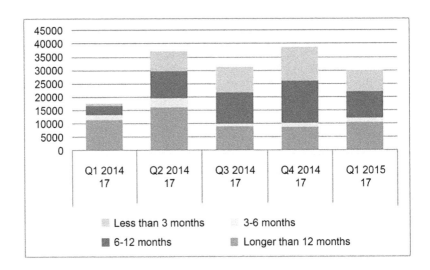

Figure 33 (Continued)

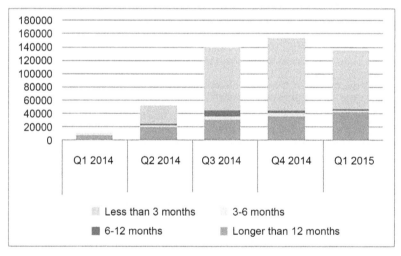

Figure 33 (Continued)

2.4 P2P platforms' total accumulated lending grows steadily

Since 2014, the amount of total lending extended by P2P platforms has increased. On the basis of the relatively complete data provided by 13 platforms, the accumulated amount of lending increased continuously in every quarter. In Q1 of 2014 the amount of accumulated loans was 17 billion RMB, but by the Q1 2015 this amount had increased to 60 billion RMB.

Almost 70% of the platforms had annual loan growth rates that exceeded 200% in 2014. It should be noted that these platforms saw quarterly growth of over 40% in accumulated loans, but by Q1 2015 this rate had declined to approximately 20%. It is unclear if the P2P industry can maintain the same frenzied growth that it had during 2013–2015.

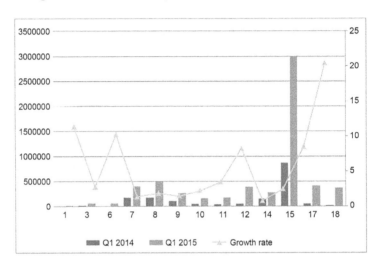

Figure 34 P2P platforms' accumulated loans (10 thousand RMB)

Note: This figure includes only the relatively complete data from 13 platforms.

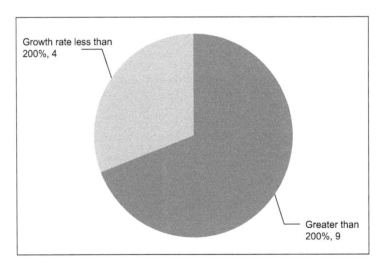

Figure 35 Growth of accumulated loans for P2P platforms (two-quarter, relatively complete data from 13 platforms)

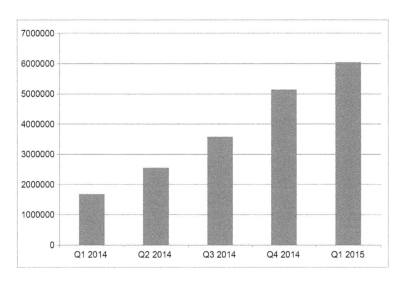

Figure 36 P2P platforms' accumulated loans (10 thousand RMB)

Note: This figure includes only the relatively complete data from 13 platforms.

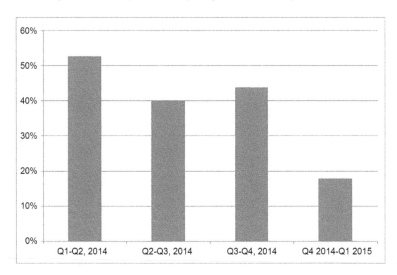

Figure 37 Growth of accumulated loans (relatively complete data from 13 platforms, %)

2.5 P2P platform loans primarily flow toward the eastern region

Traditional financial institutions in China are widely criticized for transferring funds from underdeveloped areas to developed areas, creating a situation in which poor regions lend money to rich regions. Some scholars and industry insiders believe that P2P platforms can change this scenario by attracting funds from wealthy areas to be lent to poor areas. However, by comparing how platforms in different regions distribute their loans, it is clear that P2P platforms are still accustomed to expanding their business in regions where the platform's headquarters is located; for this reason the distribution of loans is closely connected to the location of the platform headquarters.

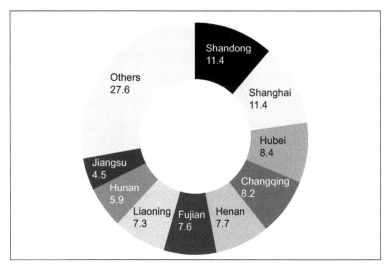

Figure 38 Regional distribution of loans for platform 10, end of 2013 (%)

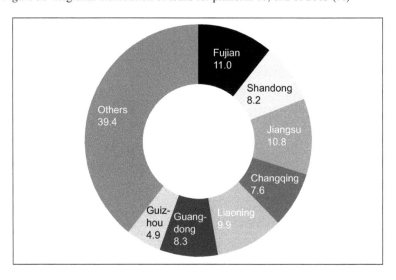

Figure 39 Regional distribution of loans for platform 10, Q1 2015 (%)

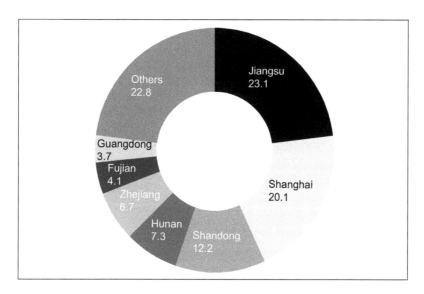

Figure 40 Regional distribution of loans for platform 8, end of 2013 (%)

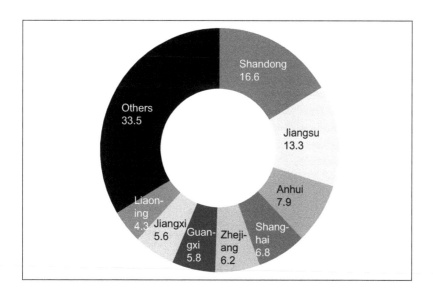

Figure 41 Regional distribution of loans for platform 8, end of 2014 (%)

2.6 P2P platform loan interest rates are high but declining

The interest rate for P2P loans is an important factor to determine the sustainability of P2P platform business models. However, it's difficult to determine the "real interest rates." On the basis of our survey, 99% of one particular platform's interest rates were concentrated between 10% and 15%, but another platform issues loans at interest rates above 15%. Though it is a reflection of different product offerings among platforms, it is also due to different billing practices among platforms. Take some platforms as an example: they charge extra service fee apart from loan interest. Therefore both interest rates and fees should be taken into consideration.

Simply looking at loan interest rates will cause confusion, but a horizontal comparison of individual platforms is to some degree reliable. It can be observed that interest rates of P2P platforms are on the decline. Platform 7 shows that 77% of the loans it gathered in 2013 had an interest rate above 15%, but by Q1 2015 not even 10% of its loans had interest rates above 15%. Loans for platform 8 were concentrated between 10% and 15%; however, the percentage of loans with interest rates below 10% increased from below 1% in Q1 2014 to almost 10%

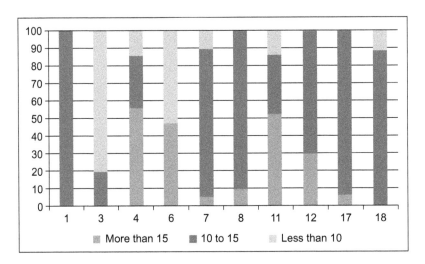

Figure 42 P2P platforms interest rates, Q1 2015 (%)

in Q1 2015. The percentage of loans with interest rates below 10% increased from 12.5% in 2013 to more than 50% in Q1 of 2015 for platform 11. Although China's interest rate has been declining since 2013, P2P platforms' loan interest rates have fallen more than the benchmark interest rate.

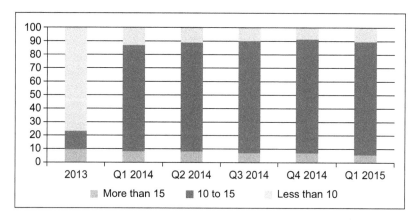

Figure 43 Interest rates for platform 7 (%)

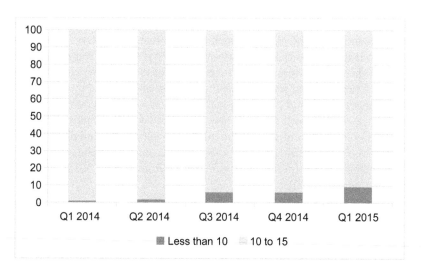

Figure 44 Interest rates for platform 8 (%)

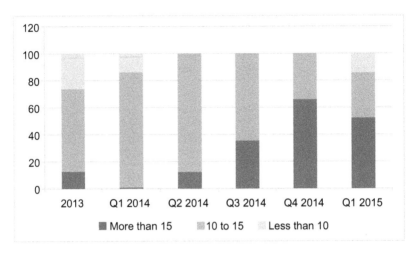

Figure 45 Interest rates for platform 11 (%)

2.7 P2P platforms have different patterns of revenue sources

When getting a loan from a P2P platform, borrowers have to pay a certain amount of fees to the platform aside from interest to investors. These fees now constitute a main source of income for P2P platforms. Some platforms do not charge fees from investors, and 100% of their income comes in the form of either service fees or account management fees paid by borrowers. Platforms 1, 7, 15, and 17 operate in this manner. Although platform 11 also charges a "withdrawal" fee from investors, fees taken from borrowers have increased from 80% of its revenue in 2013 to 90% at the end of Q1 2015. In the case of platform 14, service fees and account management fees as a percentage of platform revenue has increased from 50% in 2013 to 80% in the first quarter of 2015.

However, there are some platforms that do not excessively rely on service fees and account management fees. For example, for platform 12, these two sources as a percentage of revenue has fallen from 96% in 2013 to 56% in Q1 2015, indicating that P2P platforms have different patterns of revenue sources.

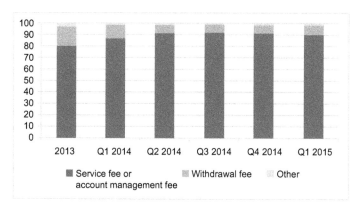

Figure 46 Billing structure of platform 11 (%)

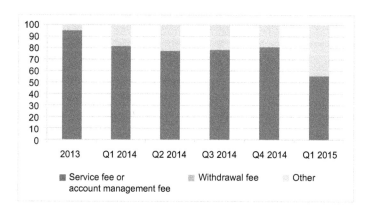

Figure 47 Billing structure of platform 12 (%)

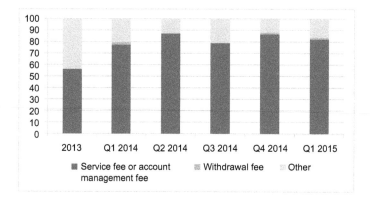

Figure 48 Billing structure of platform 14 (%)

3 Risk management of P2P platforms

3.1 P2P platforms have extended different amount of advancement

The amount of advancement provided by P2P platforms has been stable from Q4 2014 to Q1 2015. Among them, three platforms provided detailed quarterly data on advancement. The total amount of advancement made by these three platforms varied greatly, and the growth of advancement during 2014–2015 also varied. Some platforms' advancement more or less stayed stable, while those of others grew at a fast pace. However, as of Q1 2015 no single platform has an advancement to loan ratio exceeding 3%.

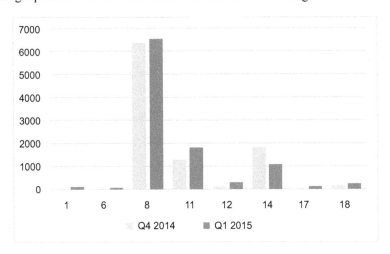

Figure 49 Amount of advancement (10 thousand RMB)

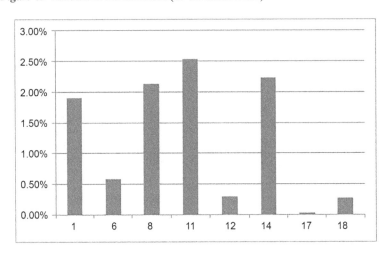

Figure 50 Advancement to loan ratio, Q1 2015 (%)

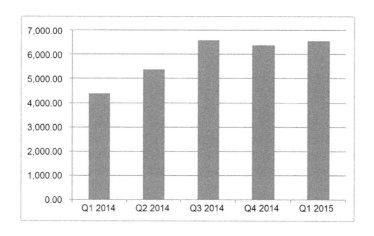

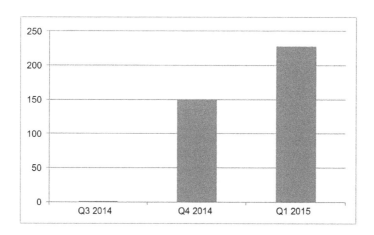

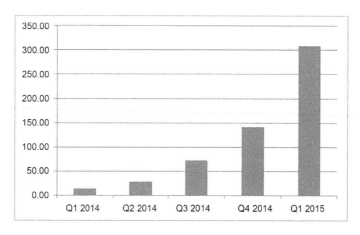

Figure 51 Advancement for individual platforms (10 thousand RMB, platforms 8, 18, 12)

3.2 Some P2P platforms have set up risk reserve funds

Forty-two percent, or 8 of the platforms in this survey maintain a risk reserve fund. Five platforms provided detailed information on how much funds were withdrawn from the risk reserve fund every quarter. The data do not show a clear trend as of the end of Q1 2015. The risk reserve fund balance of four was less than 4% of their total outstanding loans, and one platform's reserve fund balance reached approximately 10%. No matter advancements or risk reserve funds, they indicate P2P platforms are sharing credit risks and are functioning as banks rather than as information intermediaries.

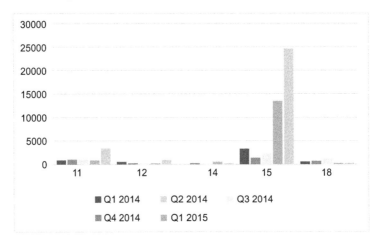

Figure 52 P2P platforms quarterly withdrawals from risk reserve funds (10 thousand RMB)

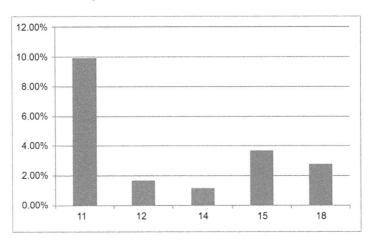

Figure 53 P2P platforms' risk reserve fund to outstanding loans ratio, Q1 2015 (%)

3.3 Overdue loans grow rapidly but are stable as a percentage of overall lending

P2P platforms have not been operating for very long. Since 2014 there has been a gradual increase in the amount of overdue loans. Four P2P platforms have provided detailed information on quarterly overdue loans. The absolute amount and growth rate of overdue loans have increased rapidly. Because of different business models, maturity structures for overdue loans on different platforms are also different. For example, the majority of platform 10's overdue loans have terms of approximately 90–180 days; however, the majority of overdue loans of platform 12 and 16 have term lengths of 30 days or less. Overall, the vast majority of overdue loans on the four platforms had a maturity of less than 180 days.

The ratio of overdue loans to total loans is relatively stable for individual platforms. For platform 10, this ratio has been stable at approximately 1% aside from its initial phase; platform 10 has maintained a ratio within the range of 1.5% to 2.5%; that of platform 15 has been stable at 3% to 4%, even suddenly shot up to 7% in Q1 of 2015.

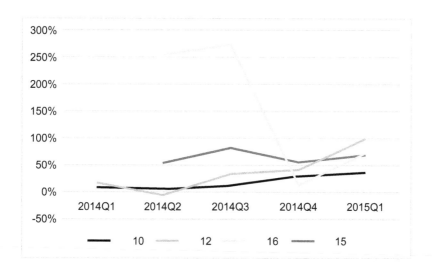

Figure 54 Quarter-on-quarter growth of P2P platforms' total overdue loans (%)

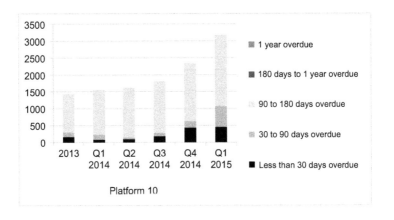

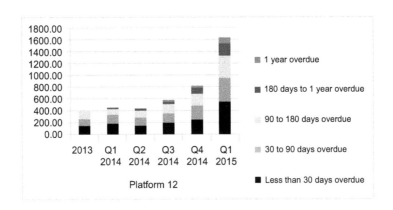

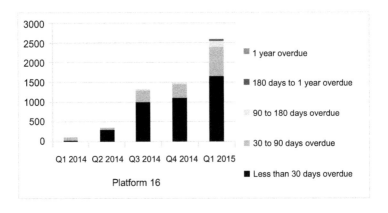

Figure 55 Structure of P2P platform overdue loans

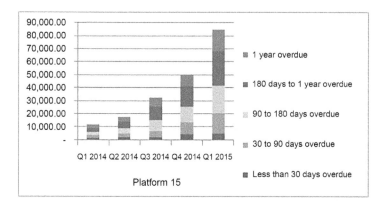

Figure 55 (Continued)

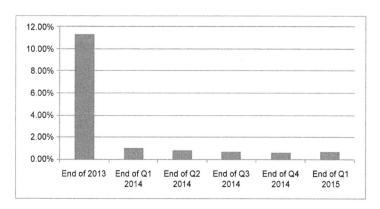

Figure 56 Ratio of overdue loans to outstanding loans, platform 10 (%)

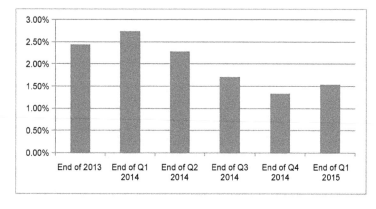

Figure 57 Ratio of overdue loans to outstanding loans, platform 12 (%)

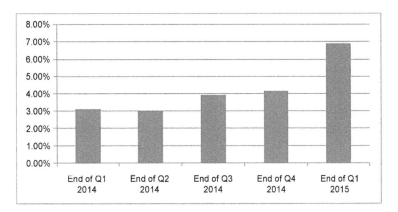

Figure 58 Platform 15 ratio of overdue loans to total loans (%)

3.4 P2P platforms are highly leveraged

The ideal P2P platform is one that simply provides information intermediary services for borrowers and lenders. It would have no obligation to repay any of the loans it matches with its own assets. However, China's P2P platforms are evolving into actual credit intermediaries. We can roughly analyze a P2P platform's level of leveraging by looking at the ratio of total outstanding loans to its asset base (net assets). On the basis of the data provided by 15 platforms, there are 10 platforms with outstanding loans that are 10 times more than their paid-in capital, and there are 7 platforms whose loans are more than 50 times greater than their paid-in capital, and some platforms have a leverage ratio of more than 200 times. It is clear that P2P platforms are highly leveraged.

If we look at the ratio of outstanding loans to net capital as a measure of leverage ratio, there are seven platforms that have provided data for their total loans as well as assets and liabilities. On the basis of the data, we found that leveraging is also very high in general, with five out of seven platforms having outstanding loans that are 10 times greater than their net assets.

3.5 Half of P2P platforms claim to have liquidity support

Liquidity risks pose a serious threat to P2P platforms. On the basis of a comparative analysis of platforms' cash holdings, current deposits, and outstanding balances of matched loans, we can see that all nine platforms that provided data have a liquidity ratio (liquid assets/outstanding loans*100%) that is above 1%, of which five platforms have a ratio above 3%. Furthermore, our survey found that over half of platforms claim that they can to obtain liquidity support from banks, parent companies, affiliated businesses, or other organizations.

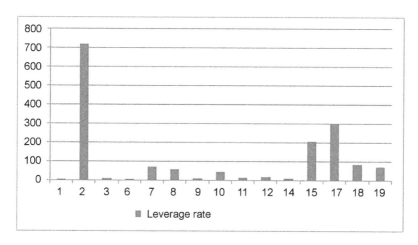

Figure 59 P2P platforms' outstanding loans to paid-in capital ratio, Q1 2015 (times)

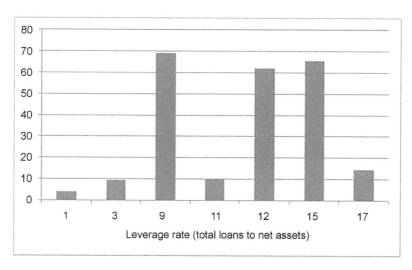

Figure 60 P2P platforms' total loans to net assets ratio, Q1 2015 (times)

3.6 A majority of P2P platforms use custody services

As an information intermediary between borrowers and lenders, whether or not a P2P platform has access to and distributes client funds is seen as an important sign to determine if the platform's operations are in compliance with rules and regulations. On the basis of the survey, more than 60% of P2P

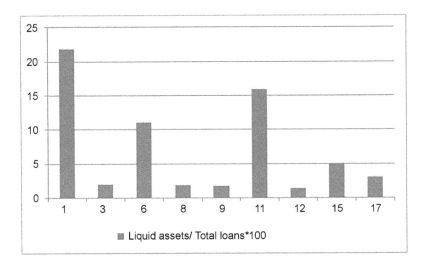

Figure 61 P2P platforms' liquidity ratio, Q1 2015 (%)

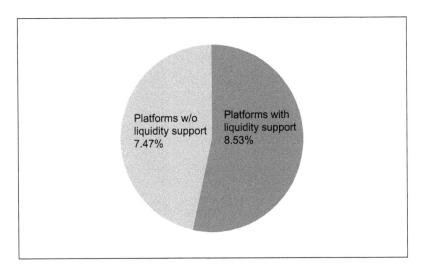

Figure 62 P2P platforms' ability to obtain external liquidity support, Q1 2015

platforms are using fund custody services. The kind of institutions that can provide custody services for the platforms include third party payment institutions (57%), banks (36%), and asset management companies (7%). Over half of the platforms use a third party payment institution as a custodian.

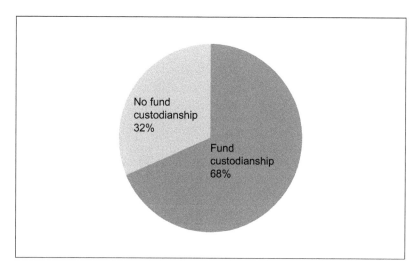

Figure 63 P2P platforms' fund custody, Q1 2015

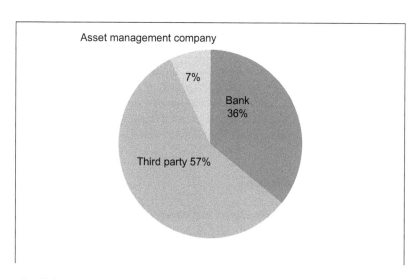

Figure 64 Composition of P2P platforms' fund custody institutions, Q1 2015

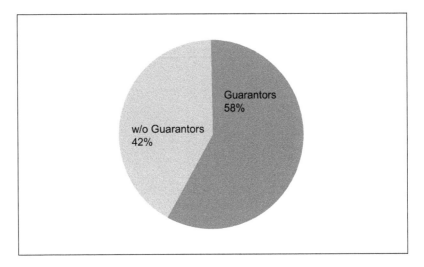

Figure 65 Fund guarantors for platforms, Q1 2015

Furthermore, over half of P2P platforms have introduced fund guarantor. There is a variety of guarantor institutions, including guarantee companies, micro loan companies, investment management and consulting companies, as well as pawnbrokers, factoring companies, and financial leasing companies. There is no major difference in the interest rate level between platforms that have not introduced a guarantor and those that have.

4 Policy recommendations

4.1 P2P regulators should clarify the nature of P2P platforms

When P2P platforms began to operate overseas, they only functioned as an information intermediary between investors and borrowers, and they did not participate in the exchange of funds, nor take any credit risk. Some Chinese platforms also took on this kind of information intermediary function. However, this survey found that many P2P platforms in China have been involved with fund transactions and have been prepared for loan losses by means of guarantors and loan provisions. By doing so, platforms have surpassed the role of information intermediaries and to some degree have become credit intermediaries.

It is for this reason that the regulators of P2P platforms should clarify the nature of the P2P platforms themselves. These two different types of platforms have different functions and should be treated differently. For information intermediaries, regulators should require platforms to have adequate information disclosure, but in the case of credit intermediaries, a reference should be made to how banks and financial institutions are regulated, with regulation requirements that are stricter than information intermediaries. There should be no space for regulatory arbitrage for these two different types of platforms.

4.2 P2P platforms should introduce third party guarantors, but there must be standards

First, parties that are directly associated with a platform and the platform itself should not be allowed to serve as an underwriter for the platform. Guarantor relationship involves three parties – the creditor, debtor, and guarantor. However, without a franchise to conduct guarantor business, P2P platforms have no contractual relationship with the debtor, and therefore are not qualified to serve as a guarantor.

Some platforms set up a company to serve as its guarantor, which is called by some experts as a "special objective company." However, this kind of guarantor is wholly owned by the platform and should be prohibited.

Second, P2P platforms can introduce third party guarantors. Guarantors are a means to enhance credit, as guarantee companies can help review the credentials of borrowers, allowing the platform and investors to obtain more information. When borrowers are unable to make payments, guarantors could share the risks taken by investors. However, the introduction of guarantor should be standardized and transparent, and the responsibility of guarantors must also be clearly defined; for example, distinctions should be made between general liability guarantee and joint liability guarantee.

Finally, platforms should perform all necessary information disclosure regarding guarantors. P2P platforms must review guarantor' qualifications and abilities and disclose all information. A great many non-finance guarantee companies in reality don't operate any guarantor services and have no relevant qualifications. Even if it is a qualified guarantee company, P2P platforms have a responsibility to confirm whether or not the specific guarantee services comply with all laws and regulations, and they must include all of this information in the P2P platform's information disclosure. This survey shows that many P2P platforms have yet to reach this level. Many platforms simply list the names of guarantee companies they cooperate with, but most do not disclose the details concerning the guarantee scheme, and there is no way to confirm the credentials of the guarantor company.

4.3 Decentralize P2P platform loans

The above statistics and analysis show that current P2P platform loans are highly concentrated. No matter if a P2P platform is an information intermediary or a credit intermediary, a high level of loan concentration is not positive for the healthy development of the platforms. For those platforms that have effectively become credit intermediary platforms, in particular, such high concentration of loans indicates a high concentration of risks. As soon as there is a large-scale loan loss, the risk reserve fund and even the net assets of the company could all be lost. In order to maintain the stability of the industry and to protect the interests of investors, it's necessary to decentralize P2P loans. Even for platforms that only serve as an information intermediary, there is the potential that their reputation could be damaged when the lenders run into trouble.

Possible solutions for regulating the concentration of loans include setting an upper limit for the size of a single loan or setting the maximum ratio of a single loan to the platform's net capital, as can be referred to the 10% cap of bank loans. Different information disclosure standards could be set for loans of different sizes, with large loans requiring more stringent standards for information disclosure.

4.4 P2P platforms must correctly implement fund custodianship

To protect against all types of fraud, P2P platforms should set up third party fund custody, but there should be a system in place to guarantee that the third party custody is legitimate and effective. Some platforms use "depository" instead of fund custody, but this is misleading to investors. These platforms place client funds or risk reserve funds in third party institutions like the bank, while still retaining the right to control the funds, which means there actually is no real fund custodianship. Steps should be taken to guarantee the efficacy and legitimacy of third party custody, which is of great implication to the safety of investor's assets.

4.5 Promote the development of the credit reporting system
with comprehensive regulation

P2P platforms should be permitted to link up with the central bank's credit reporting system as soon as possible. Without support from external credit reporting agencies, P2P platforms typically set up their own service to perform credit investigations, which is one of the reasons that the operating costs for P2P platforms is so high (including finding clients, operations, and marketing). As P2P platforms are not officially recognized entities, they are not allowed to link up with the central bank's credit reporting system. Relevant regulations and standards for including P2P platforms in the central bank's credit reporting system should be released as fast as possible.

The development of commercial credit reporting agencies should be supported. Even if the central bank opens up its credit reporting system to P2P platforms, there will still be many difficulties. The speed at which they are included and the flexibility of the system will not be able to meet the demands of P2P platforms, so commercially run credit reporting agencies can partially make up for this defect in the system.

Self-regulating industry organizations can also play a role in encouraging P2P platforms to share data. For both the central bank credit reporting system and commercial credit reporting system, P2P platforms cannot just use data from the credit reporting system without sharing their own data. Based on a survey of a credit company with central bank background, this company's Internet finance credit reporting system has already included several hundred P2P platforms, but it only has hundreds of thousands of personal entries available, which is not as big as the data held by one large P2P platform. This shows that many platforms have yet to report their data to the system, and they are just selectively reporting some of the data.

4.6 P2P platforms should have a unified and standardized information disclosure system

There should be high standards set up for P2P platforms' information disclosure. While we were conducting this survey, some P2P platforms directly rejected our requests for data. In fact, any financial institution is required by law or regulation to disclose such data. As Internet finance information intermediaries, virtually all investors can look for investment opportunities on a P2P platform. For this reason, P2P platforms should conduct rigorous information disclosure. The standards for disclosure should refer to those of listed companies and commercial banks. Strict information disclosure is a prerequisite for investors to take responsibility for their gains and losses.

Information disclosure for P2P platforms should be unified and standardized. Our survey observed that P2P platforms usually hype the scale of their loans as a way to promote their services. However, a big problem with this kind of information disclosure is that it lacks a unified standard. For example, the platforms always use the total amount of loans they have accumulated after establishment as an important operational benchmark. This is okay for a company that is just starting out, but for a platform that has been running for some time, its information disclosures should be focused on the yearly or quarterly accumulated loans and outstanding loans. Annual reports of P2P platforms should follow a unified template issued by a regulator or an industry organization to increase horizontal comparability.

Finally, there should be a soft restriction on capital adequacy ratio through information disclosure. Without hard restrictions, such as restrictions on leverage ratio, forcing a soft restriction on capital adequacy ratio through information disclosure is an effective way to protect consumers. By mandatory disclosure of information, such as a balance sheet, a profit report, cash flow, accumulated loans, and loan structure, we can build up soft restrictions on a platform's capital adequacy ratio, and investors can judge for themselves if the platform's promises or implicit promises are reliable.

Afterword

Since 2013, the P2P industry has developed quickly, but it is still an emerging industry. Official data on its development is lacking, and the data and analysis available on the market vary in quality. As a non-governmental professional think tank, data collection is a big obstacle to this research. It's greatly appreciated that nearly 20 P2P platforms provided us their precious data for this study. All analysis in this report is the result of our independent study; we are responsible for all views and errors in this report. Given that a unified information disclosure system for the P2P industry has yet to be established, we have withheld the sources of the data to protect the interests of the individual platforms. Our study is aimed at the common issues of the whole industry, not a commercial review of any single platform.

As the P2P industry is still in its startup stage, a lot of information is redundant or even contradictory, and our own research abilities are limited, there's still a lot of room for progress. We look forward to receiving feedback with hope that in the future we can make a more scientific report to contribute to the development of this industry.

Index

For Product Safety Concerns and Information please contact our EU
representative GPSR@taylorandfrancis.com
Taylor & Francis Verlag GmbH, Kaufingerstraße 24, 80331 München, Germany